Easy Mandalas

Copyright: Published in the United States by Alana Duff
Published January 2017
ISBN-13: 978-1542680004
ISBN-10: 154268000X

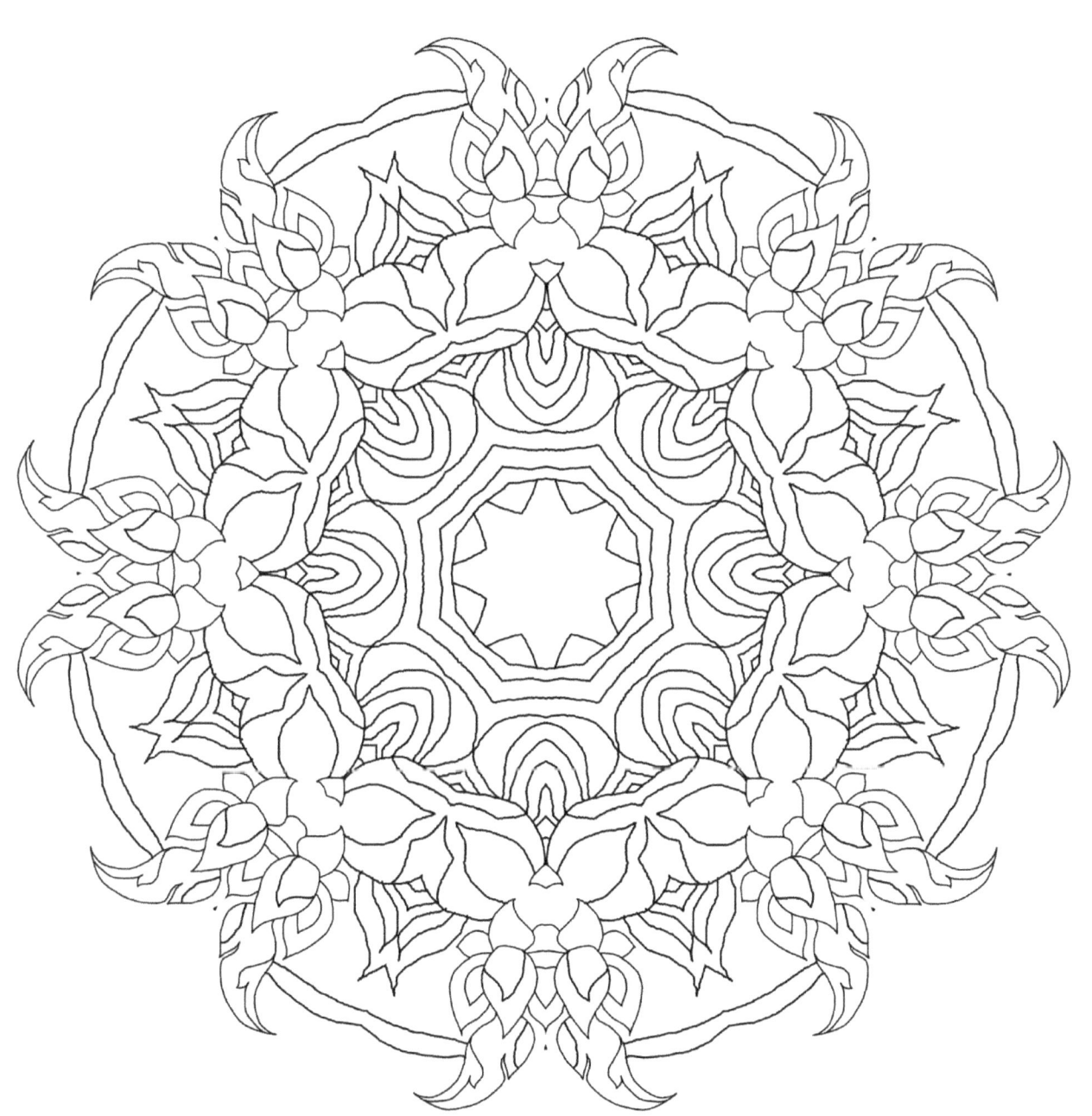

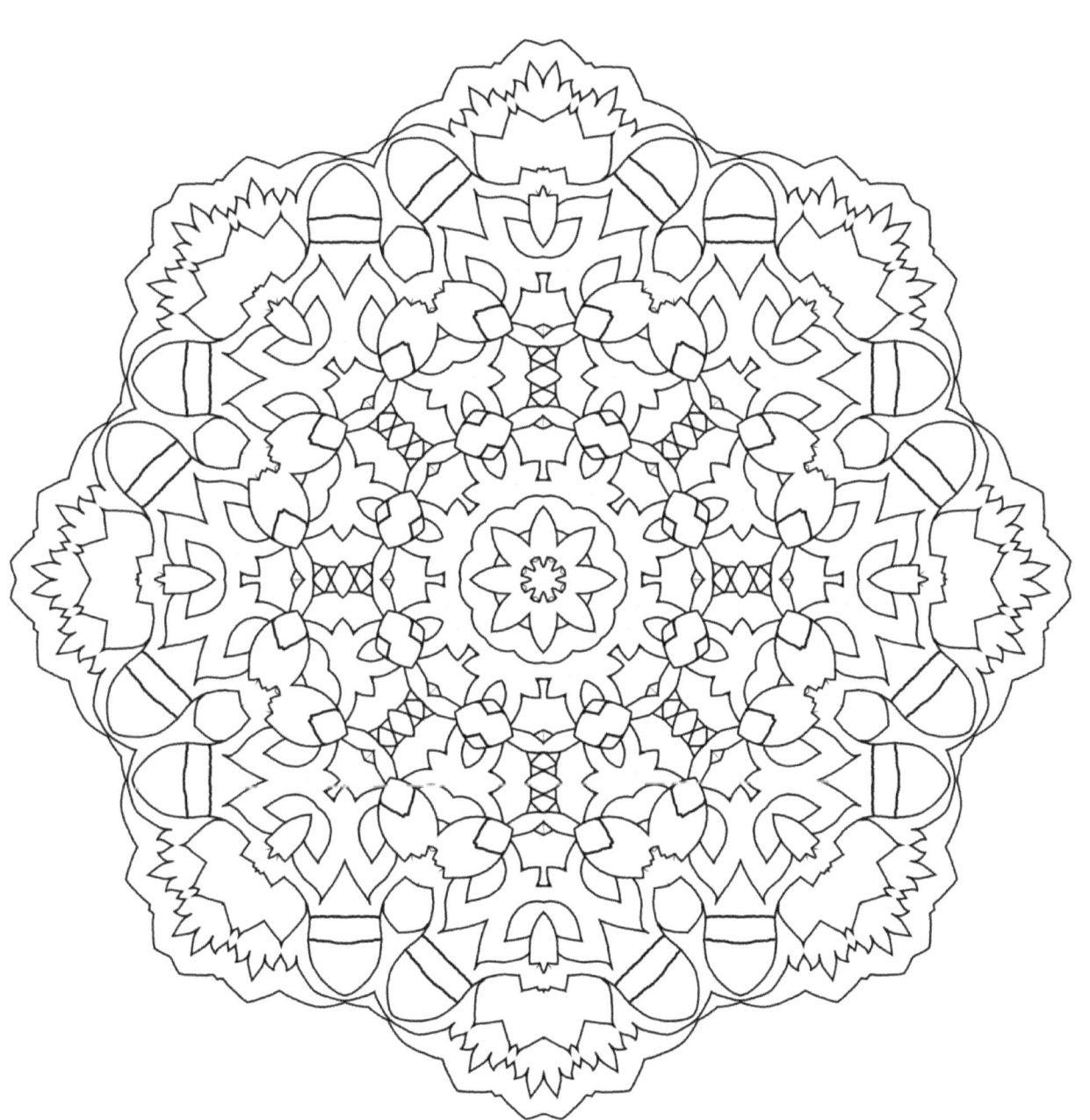

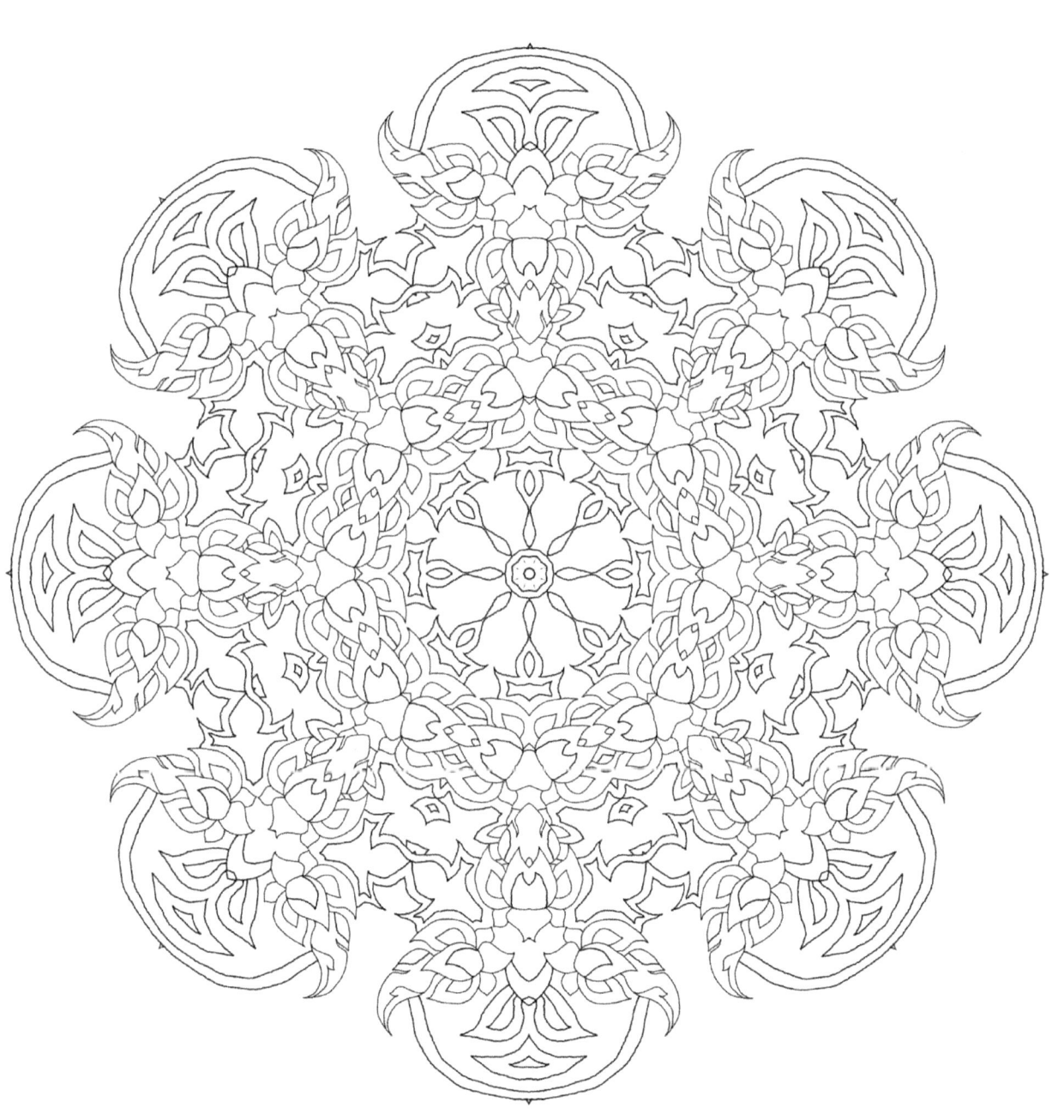

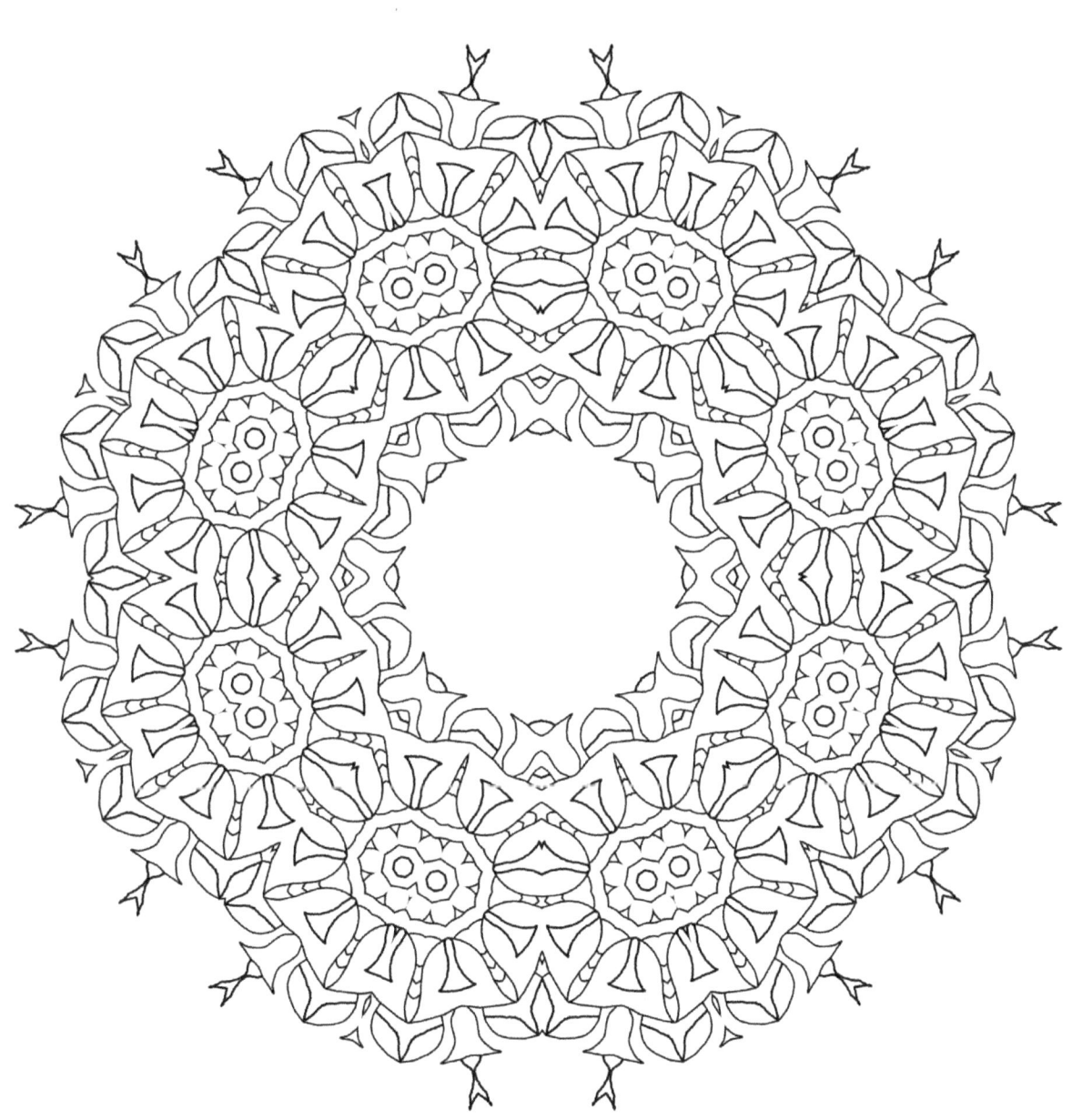

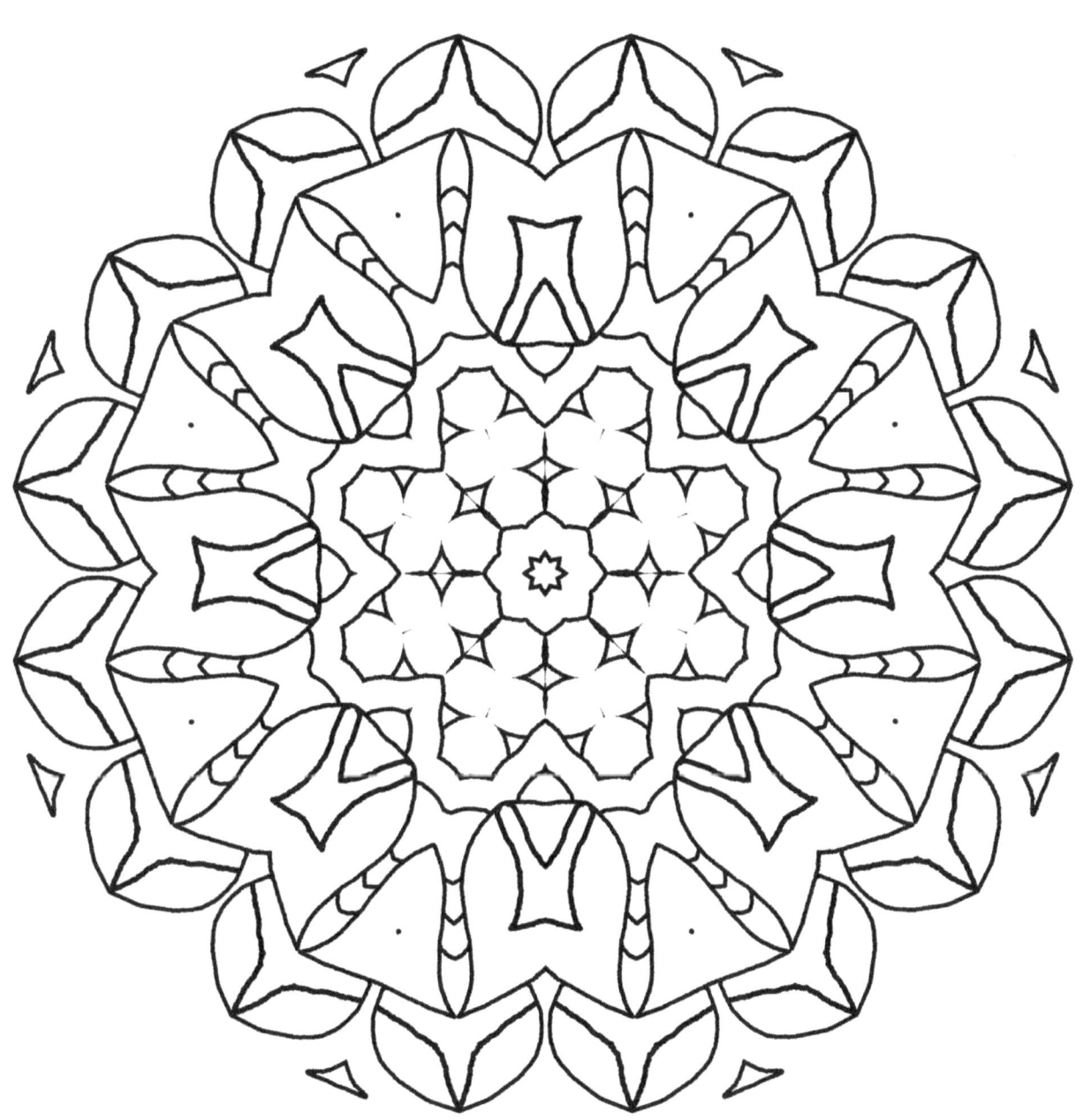

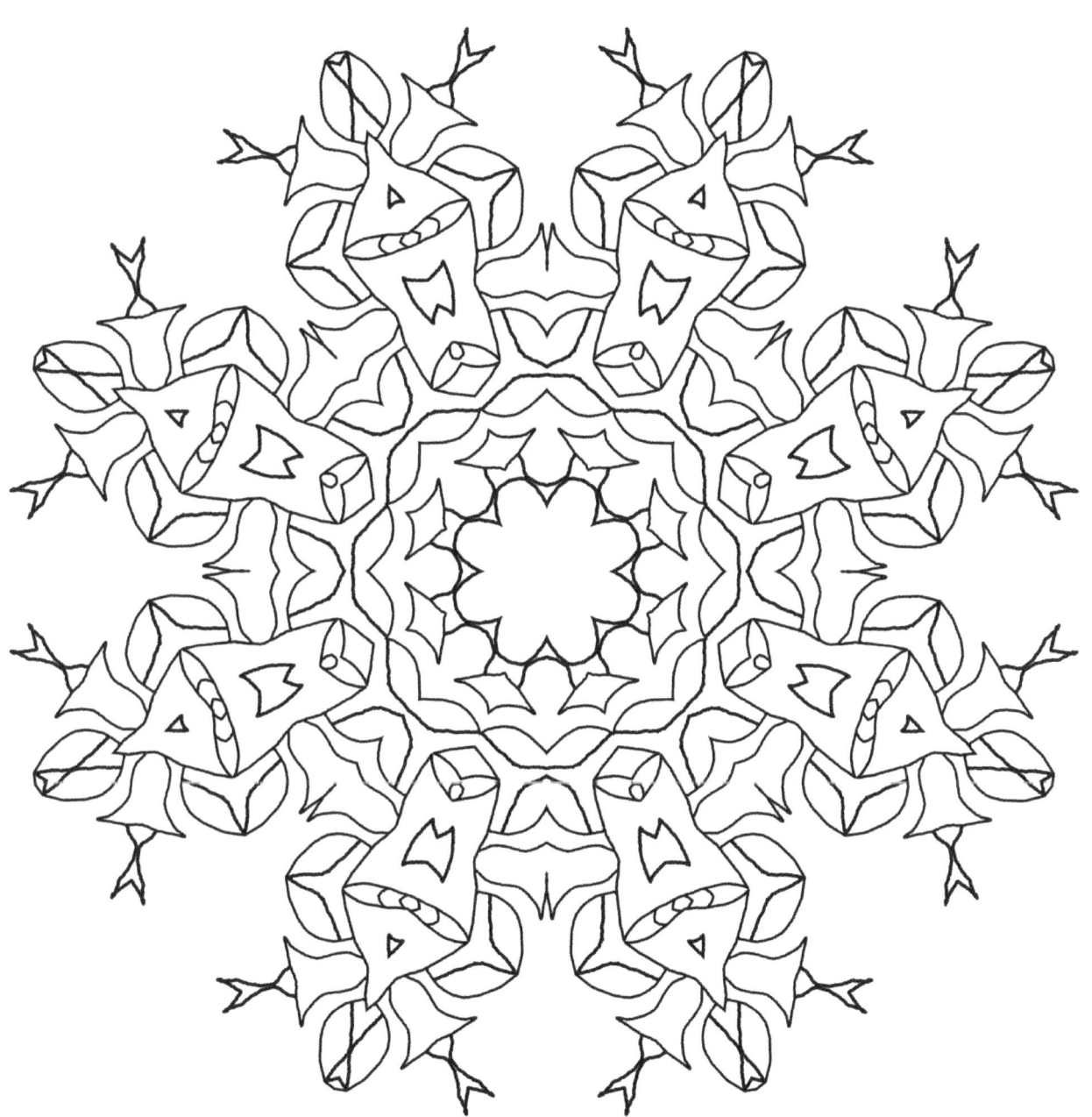

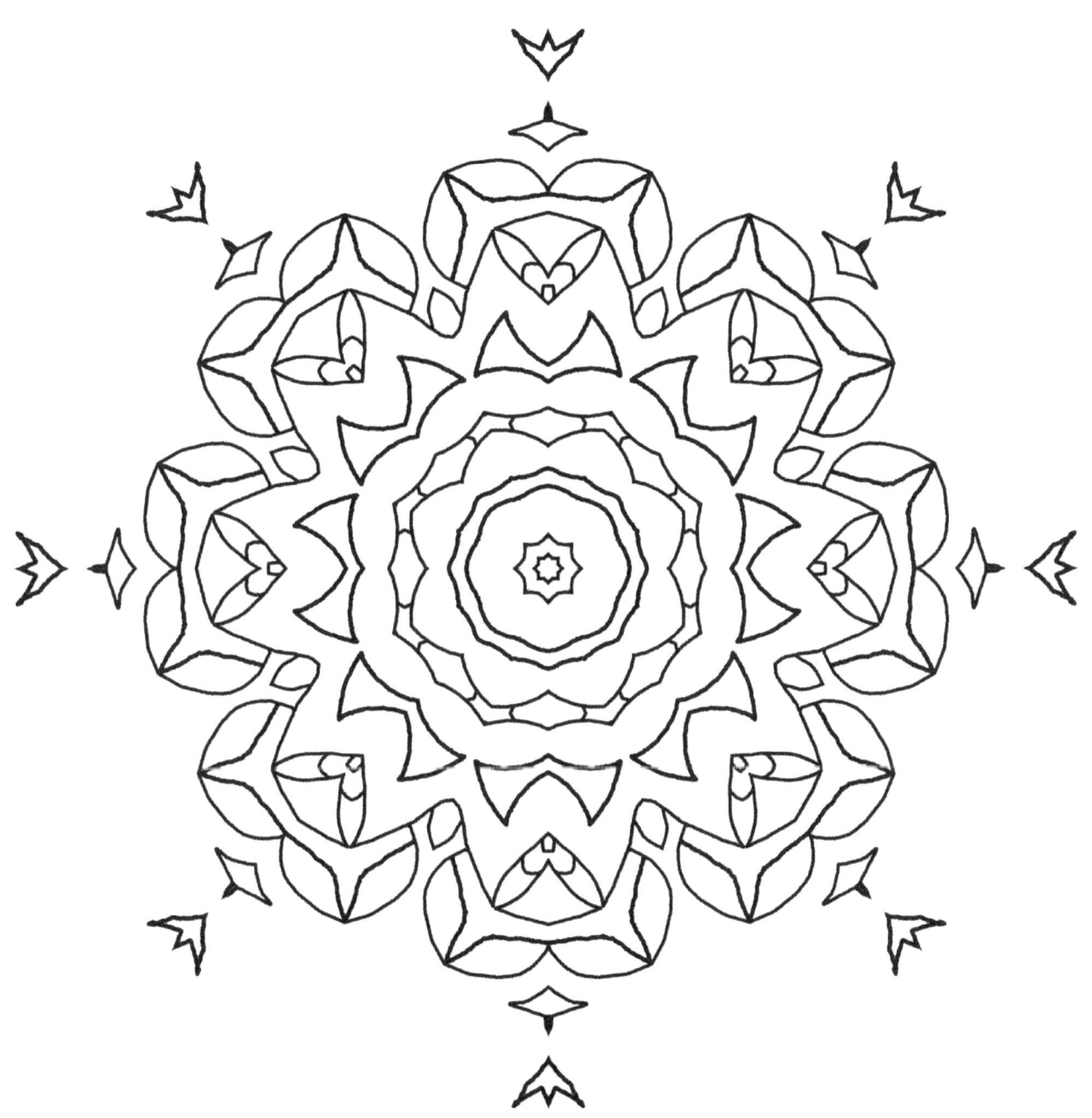

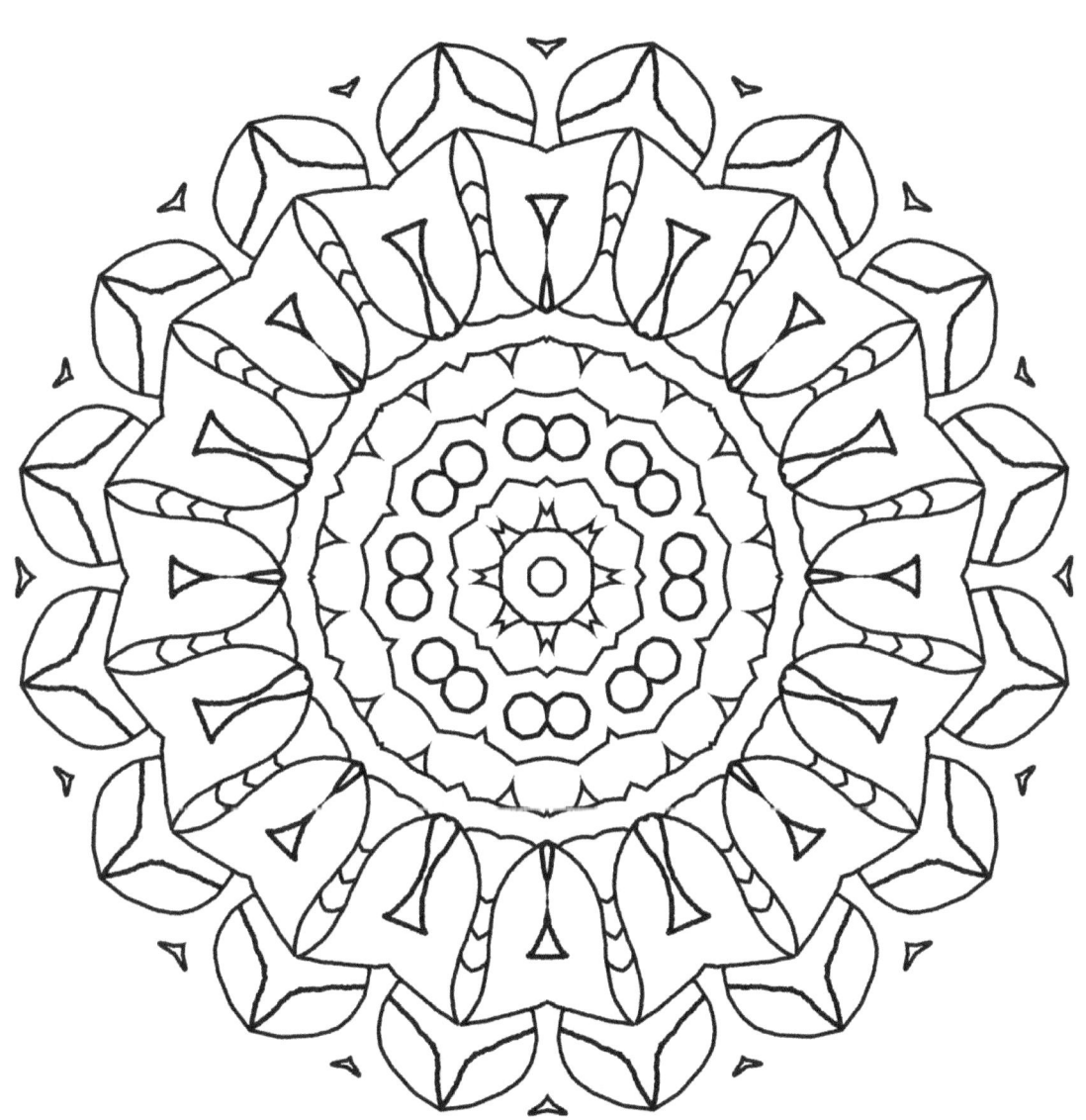

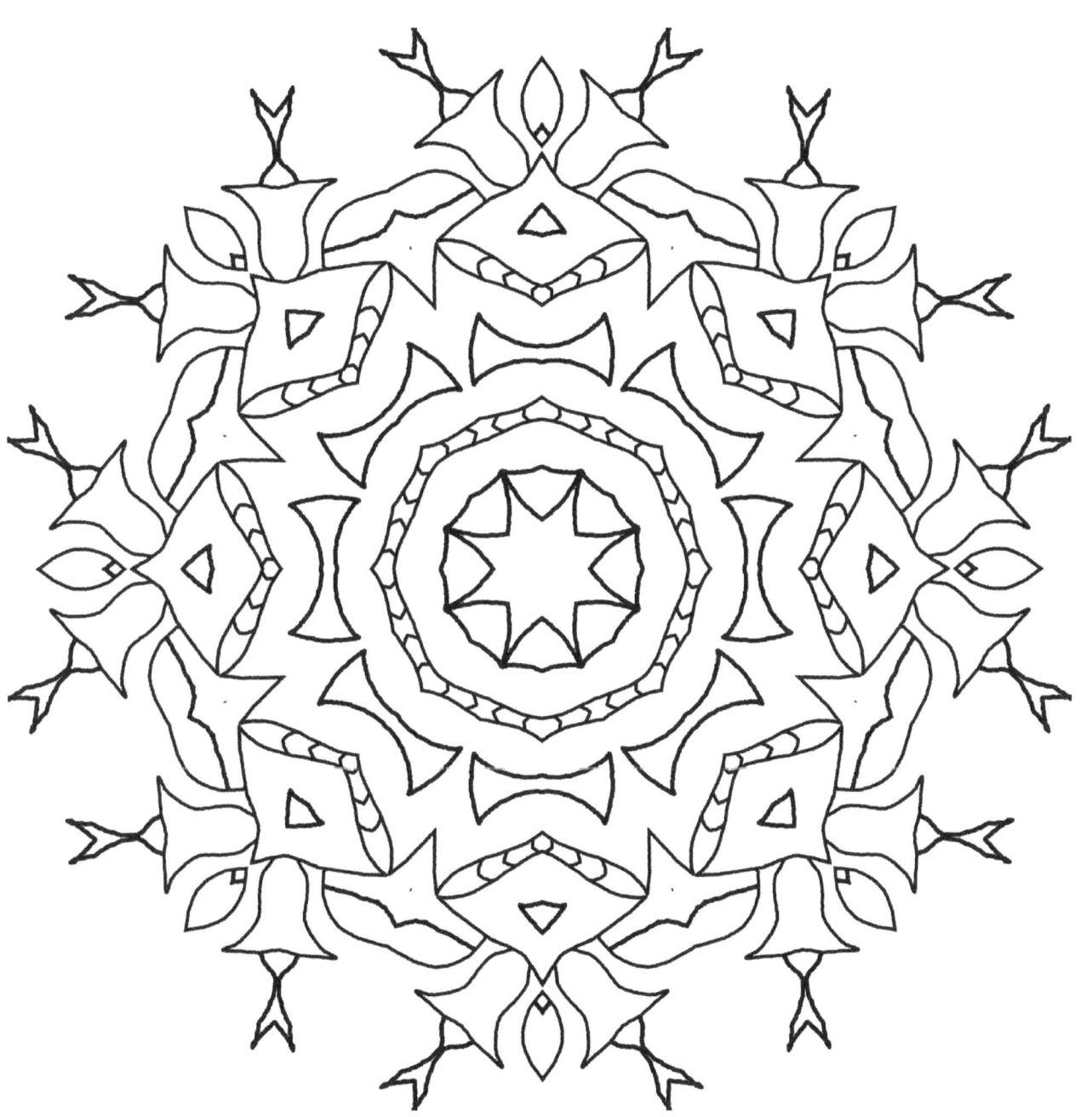

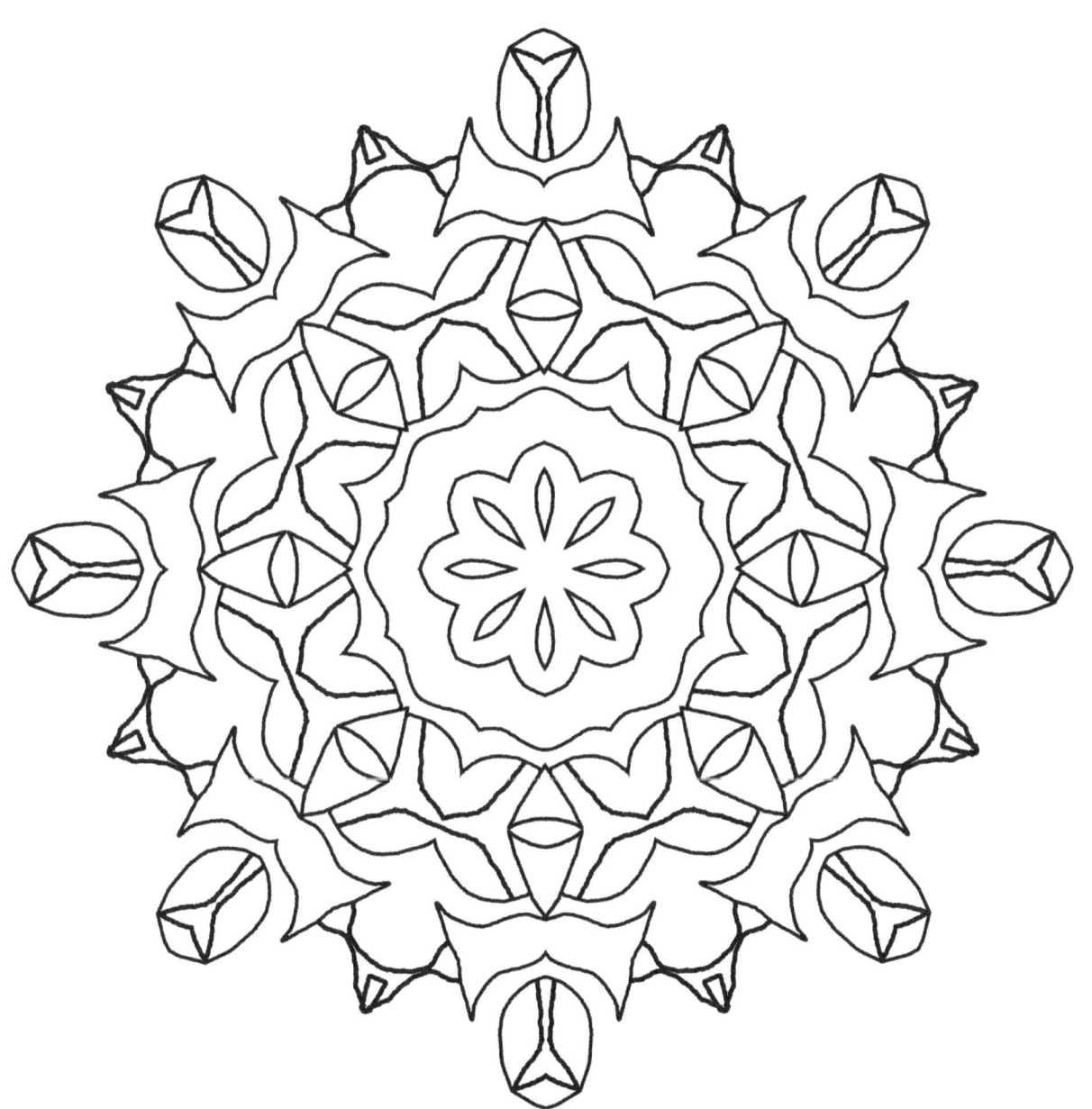

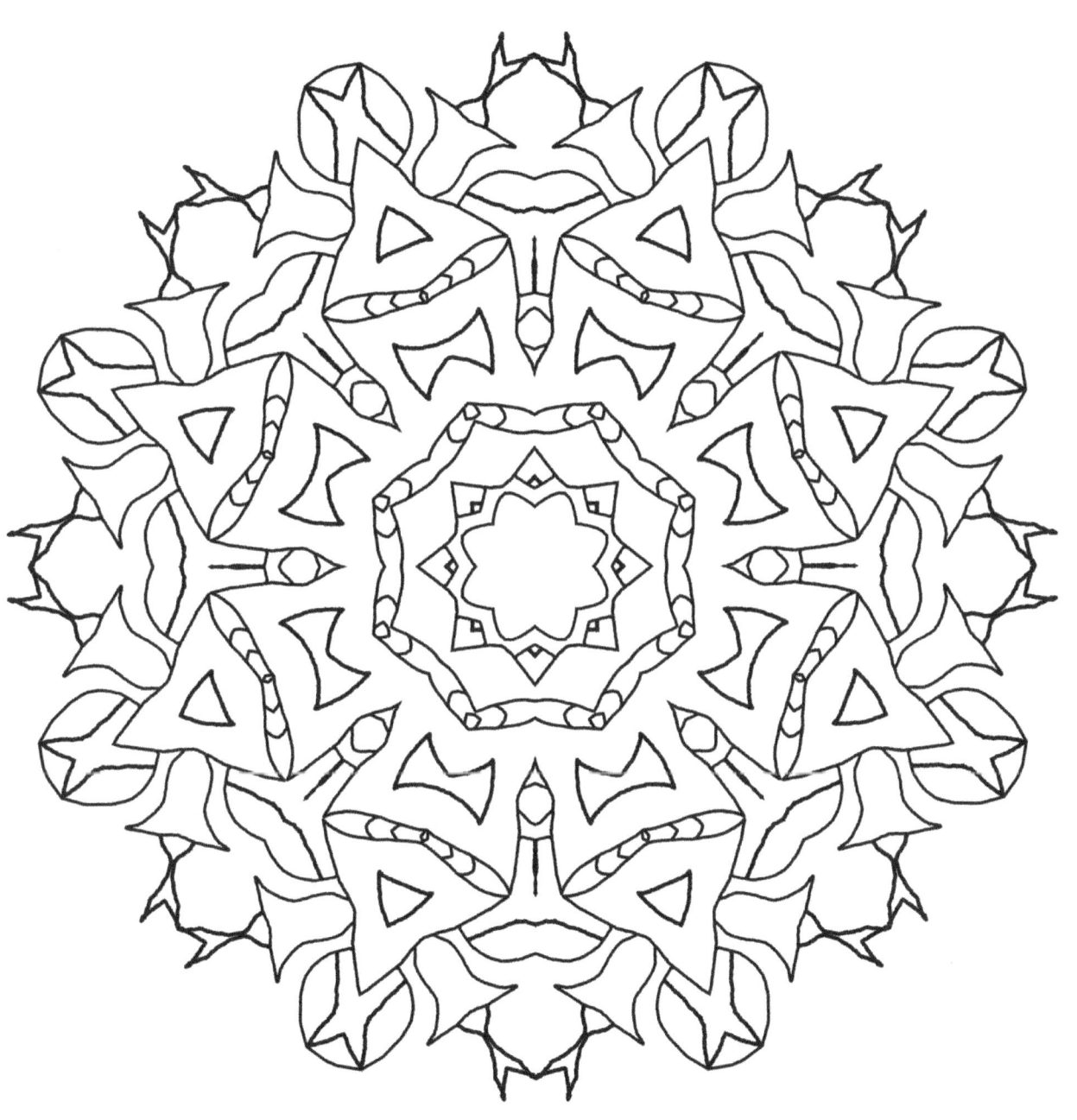

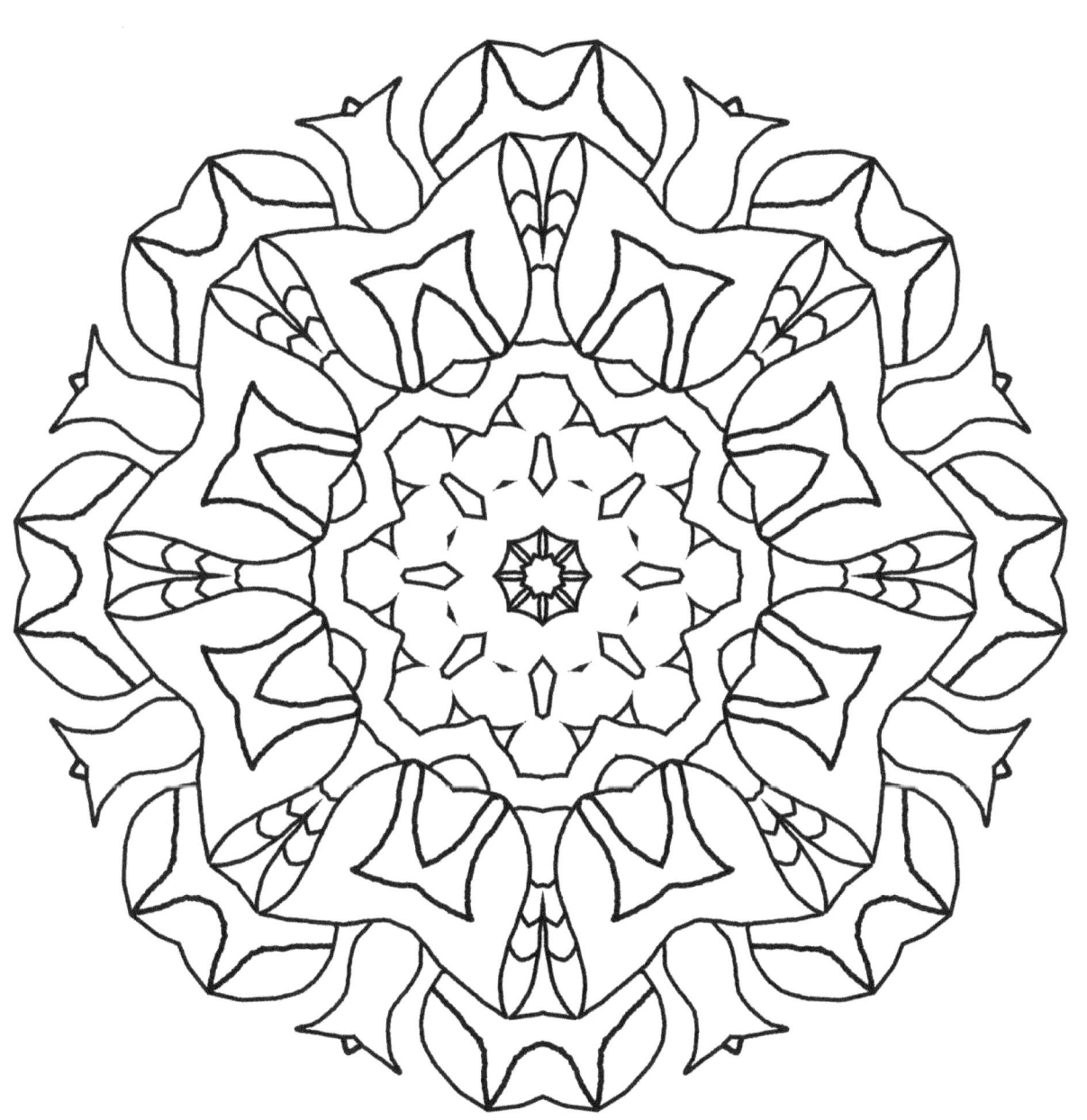

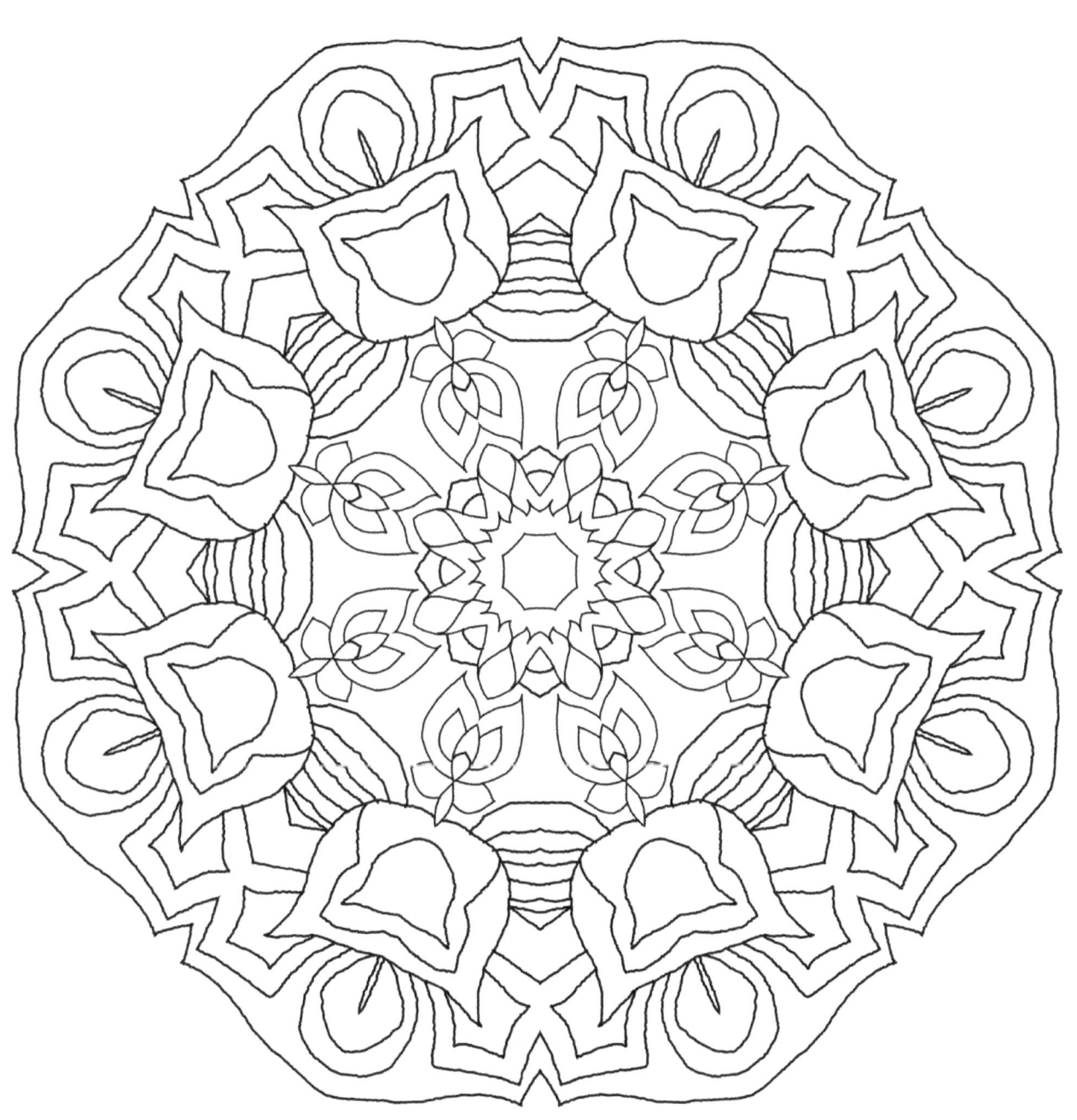

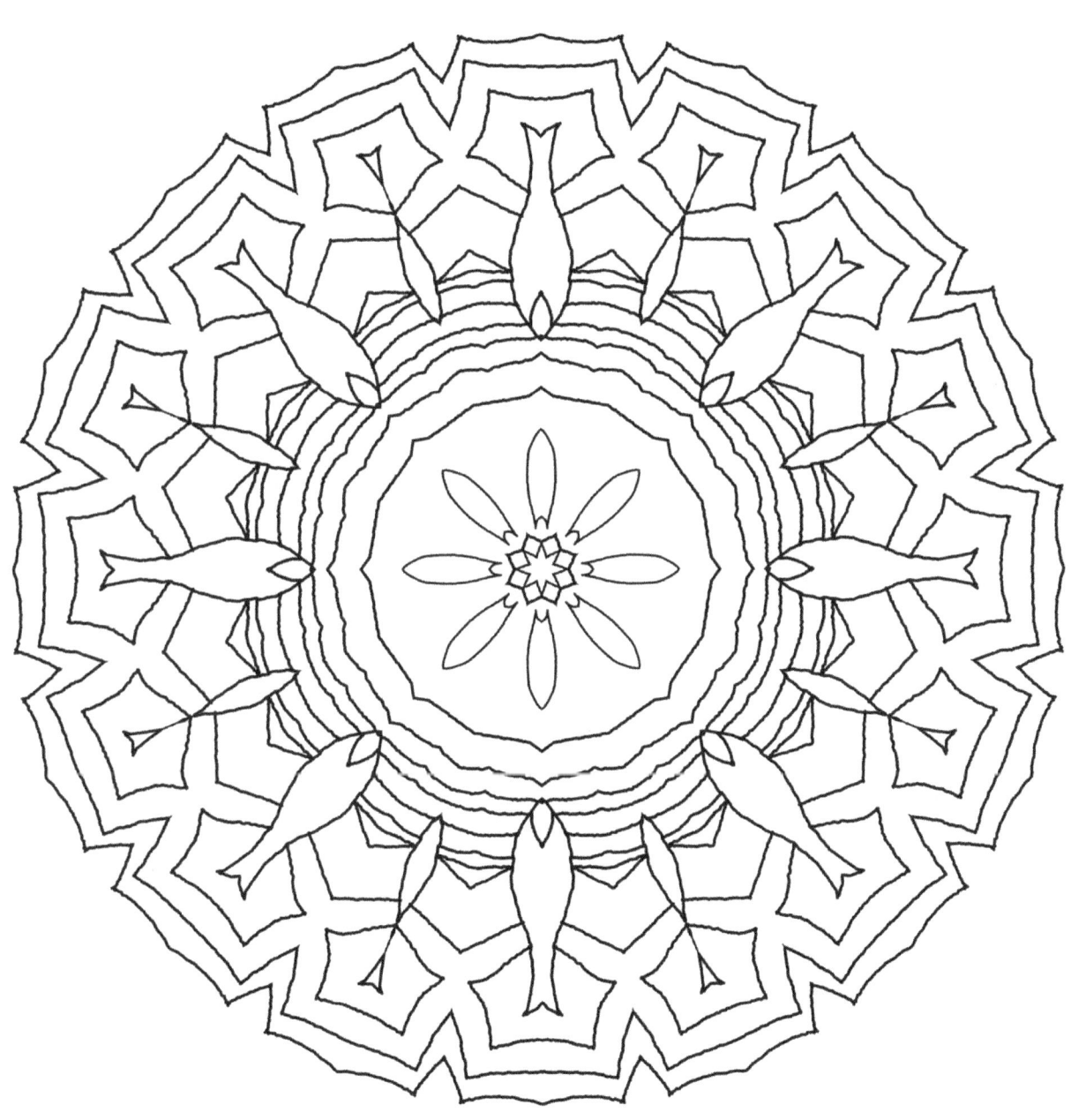

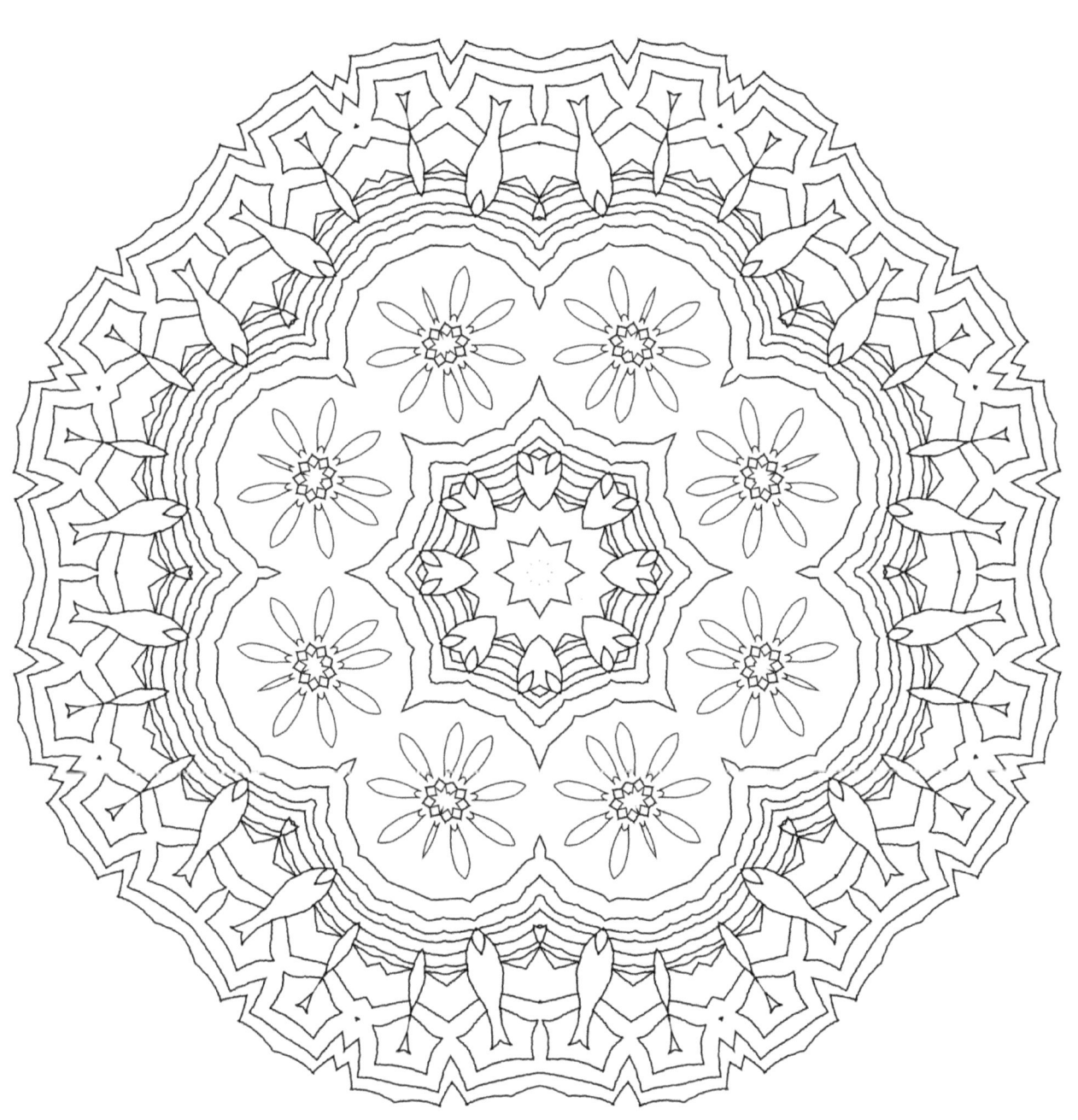

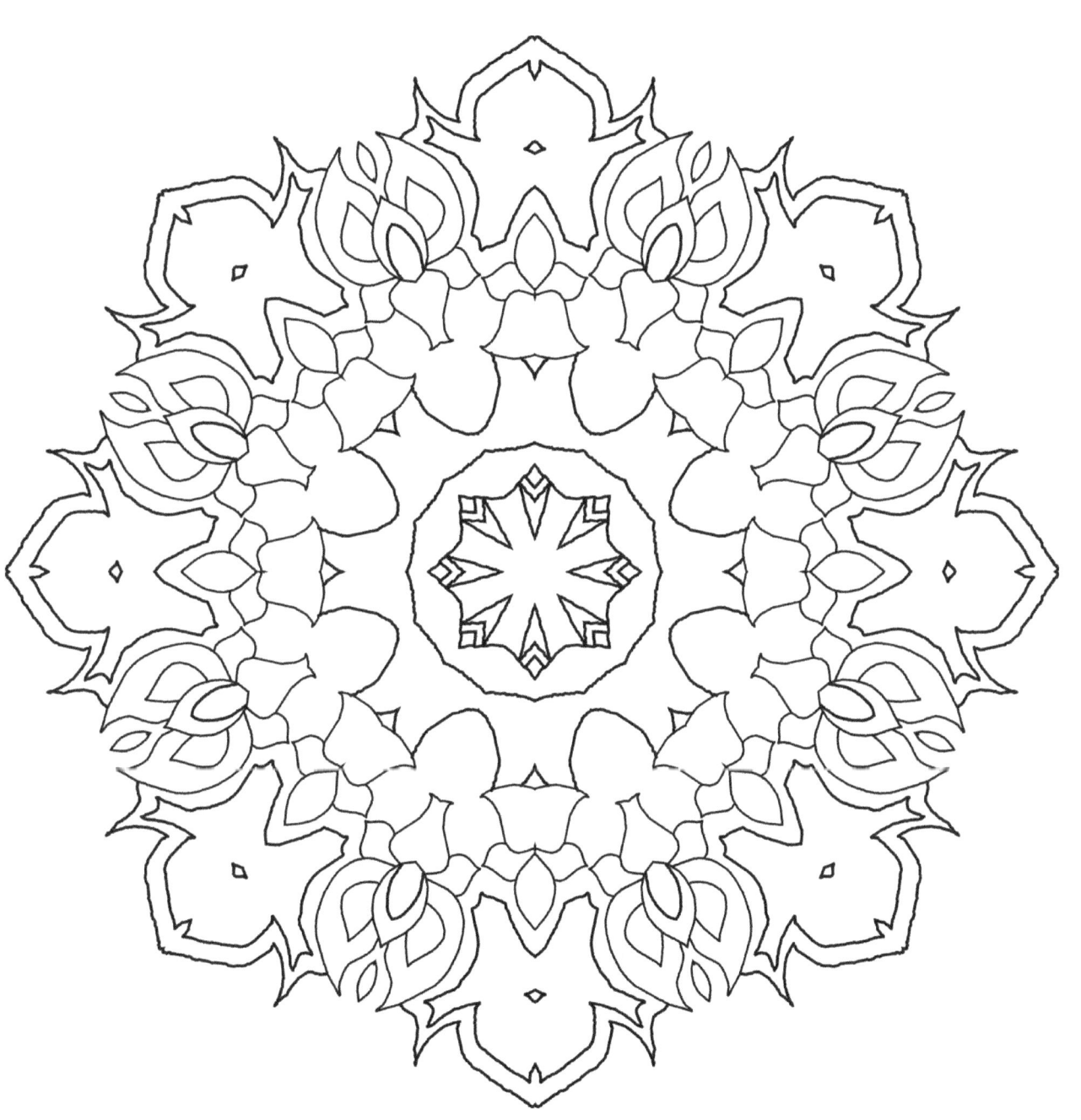

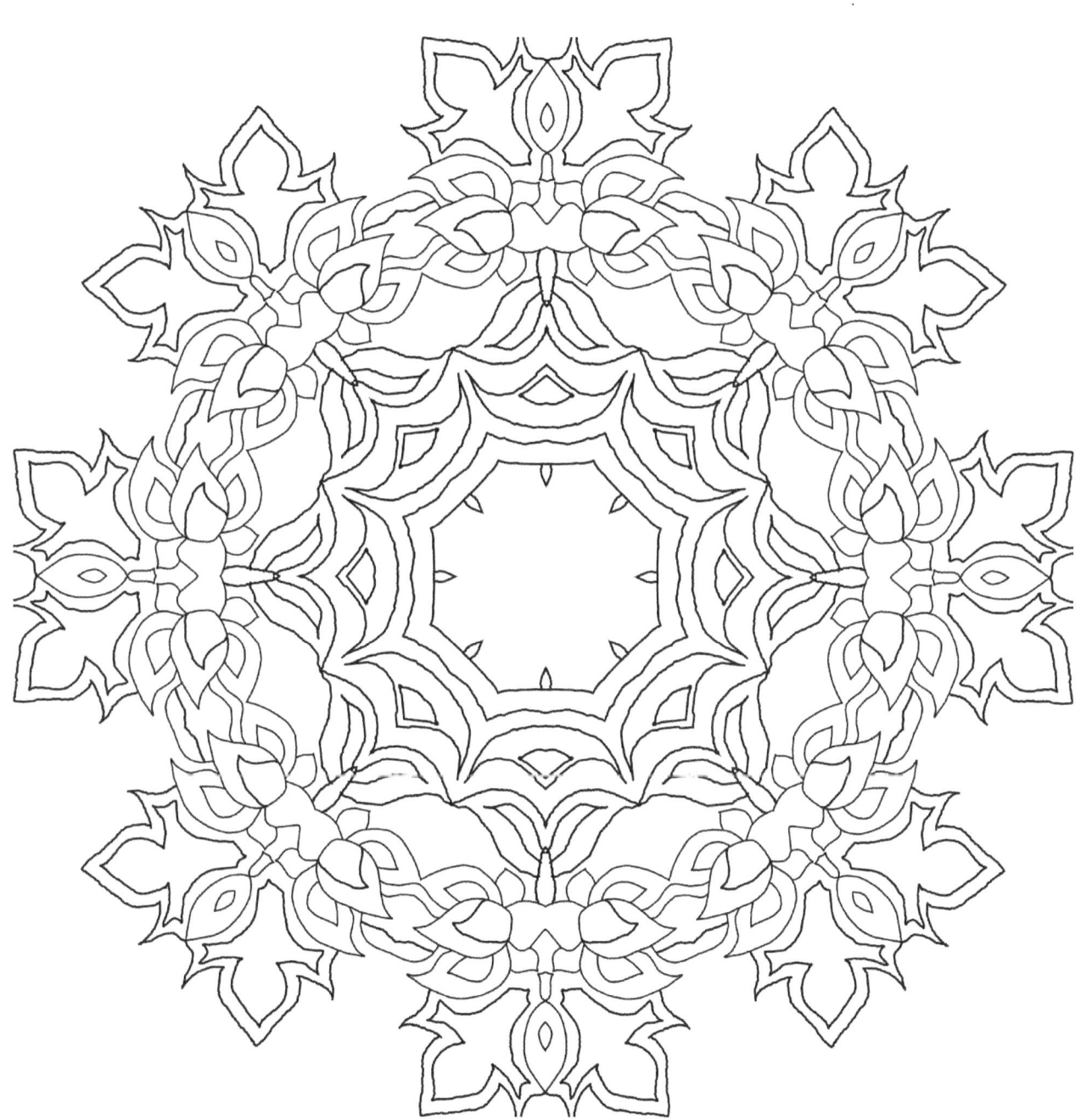

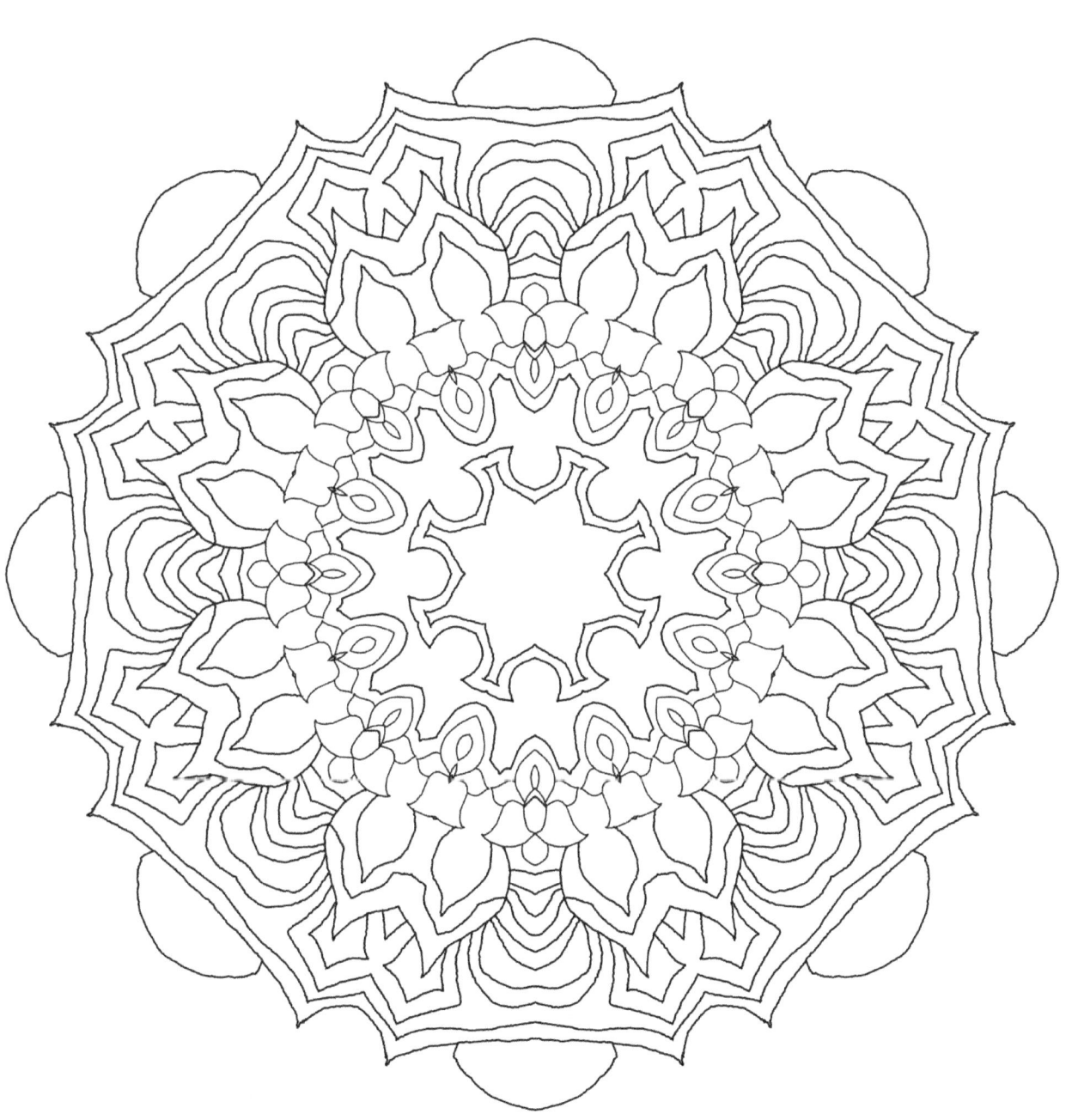

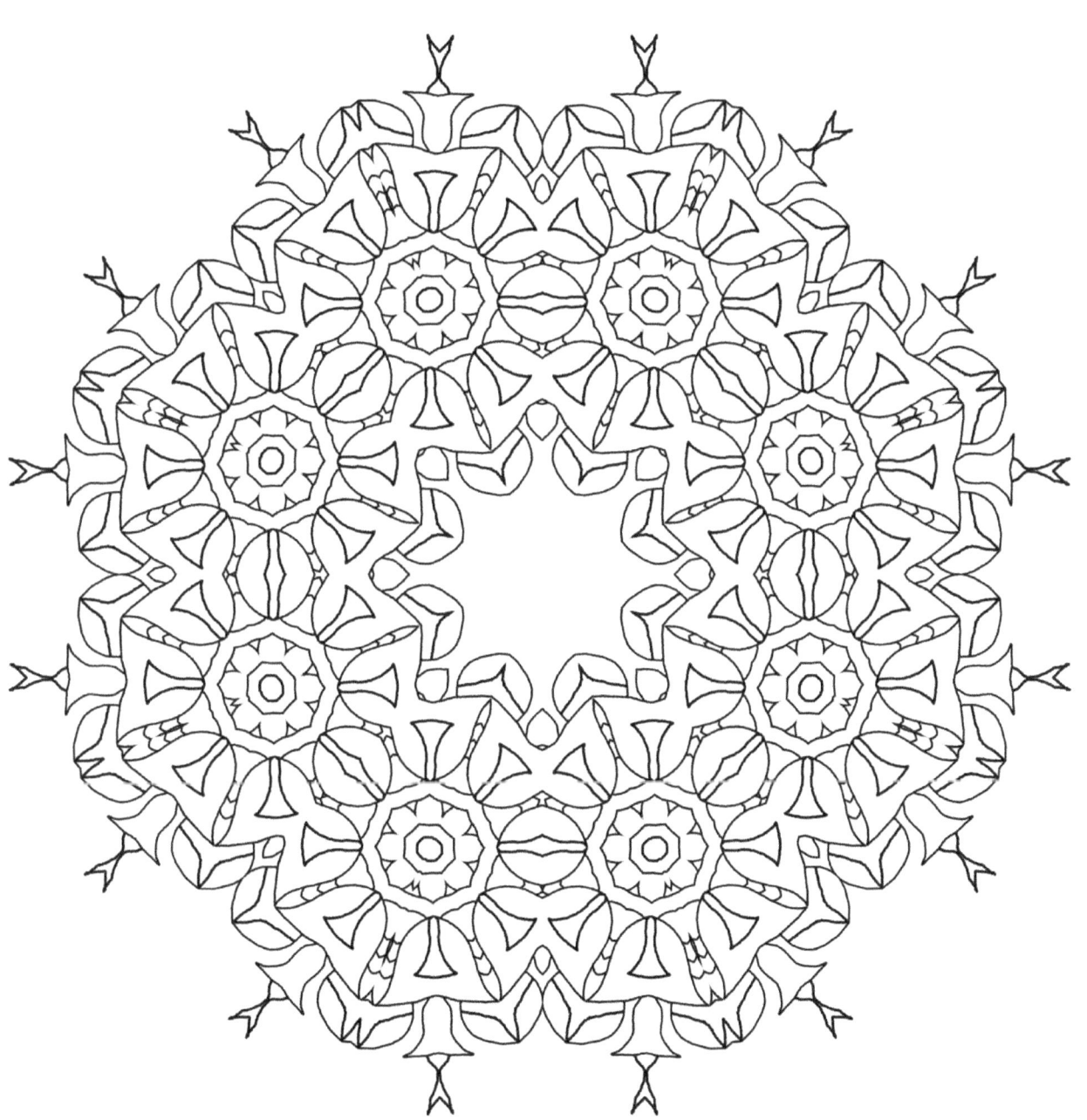

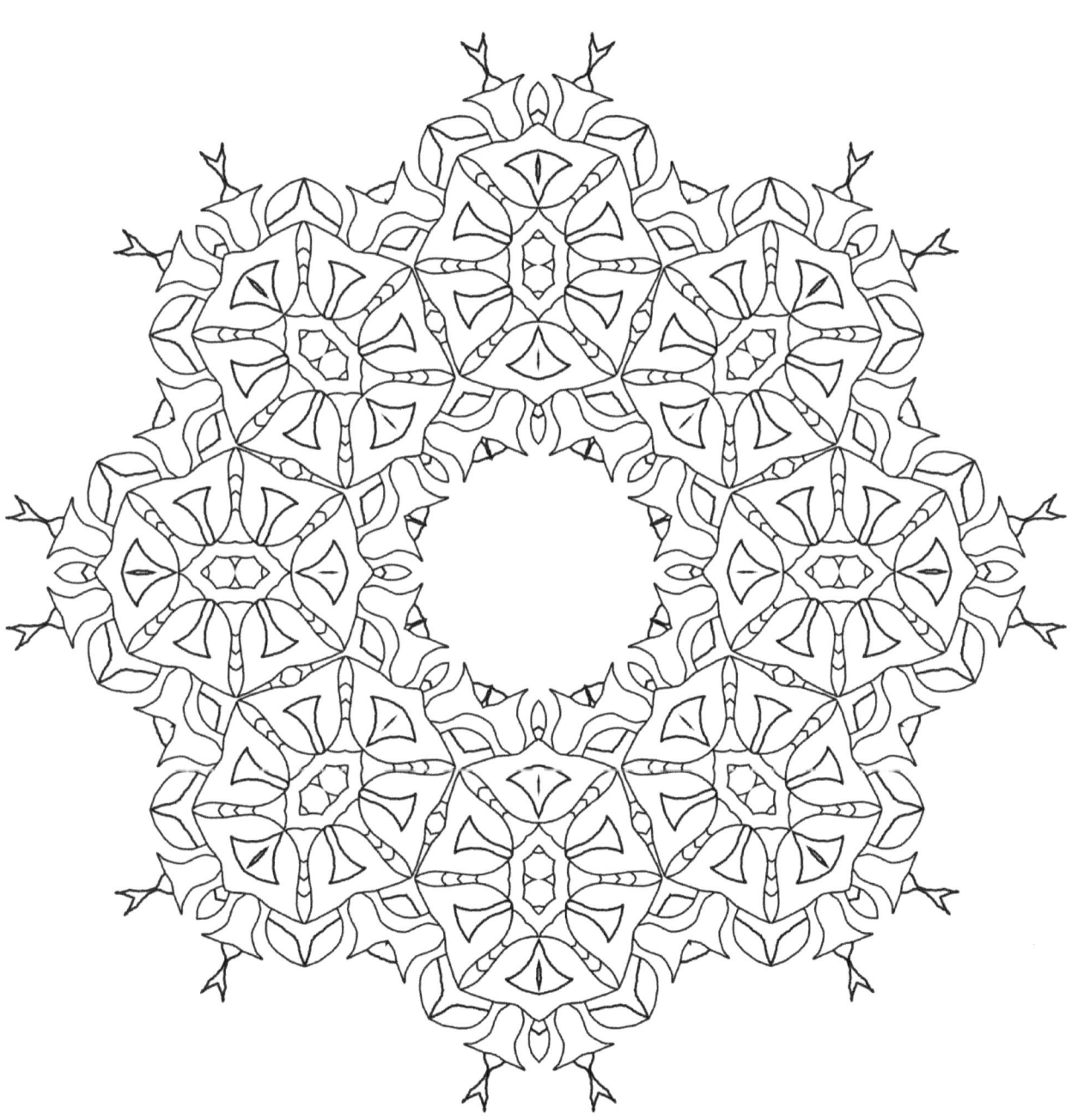

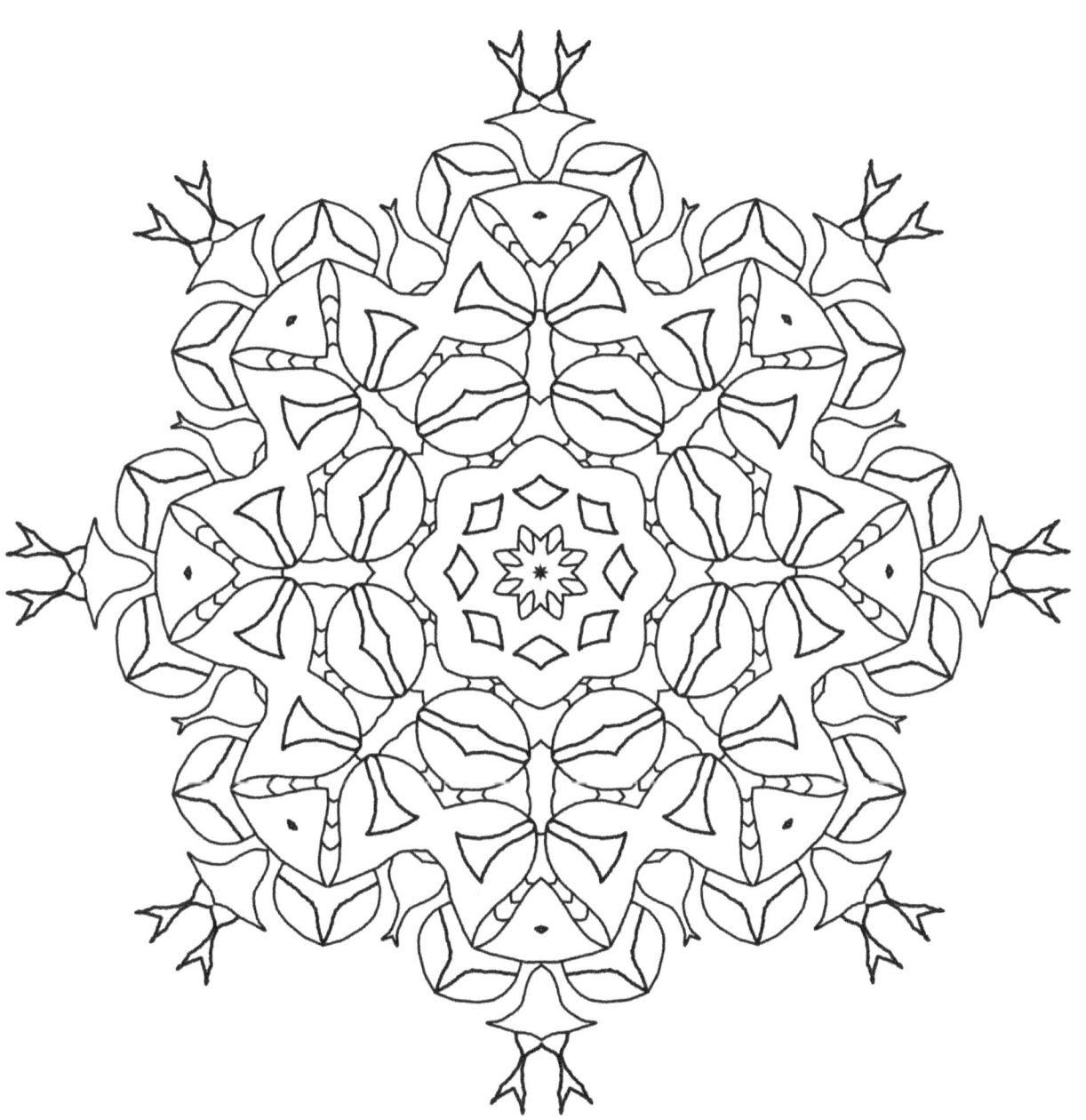

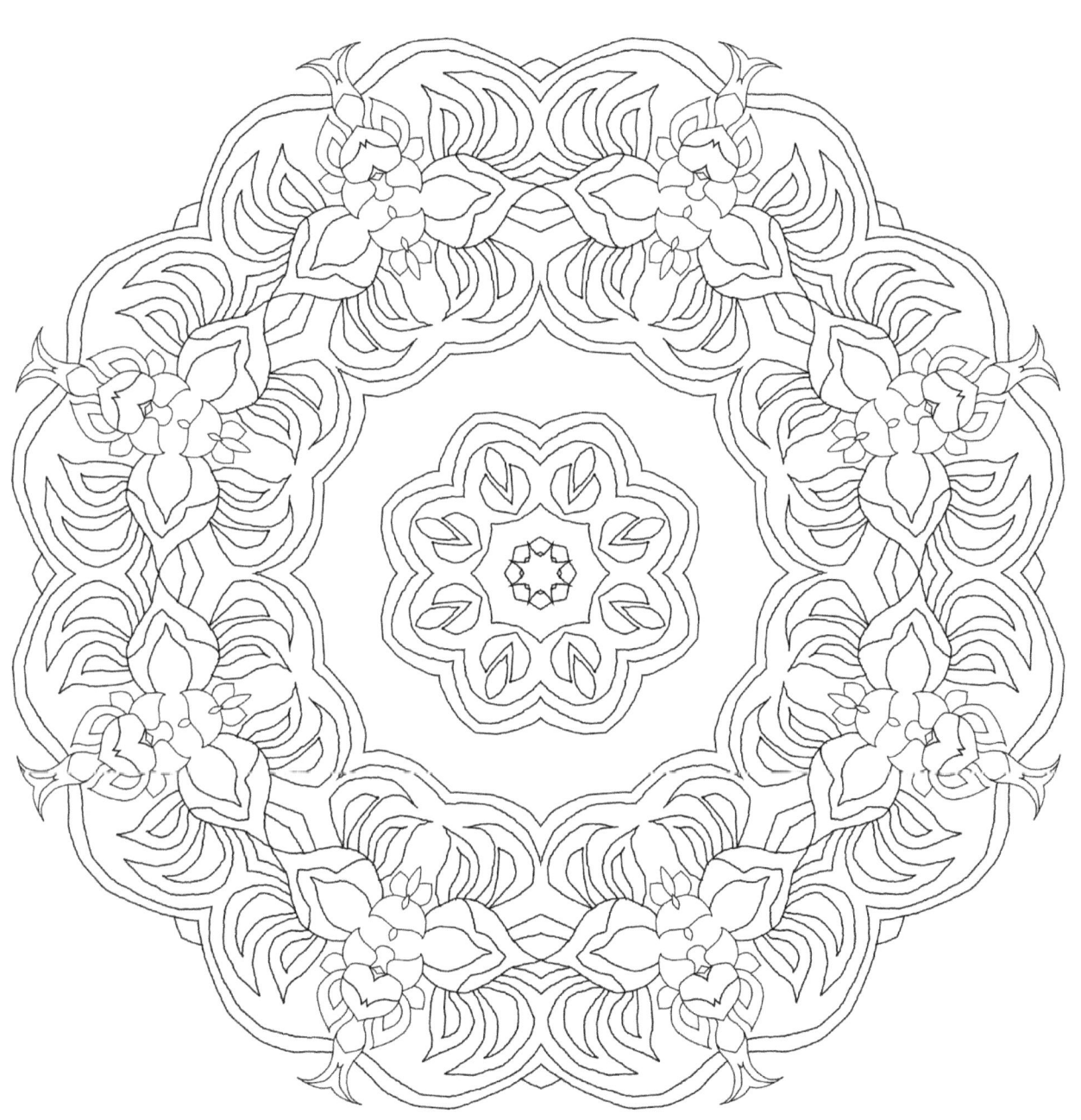

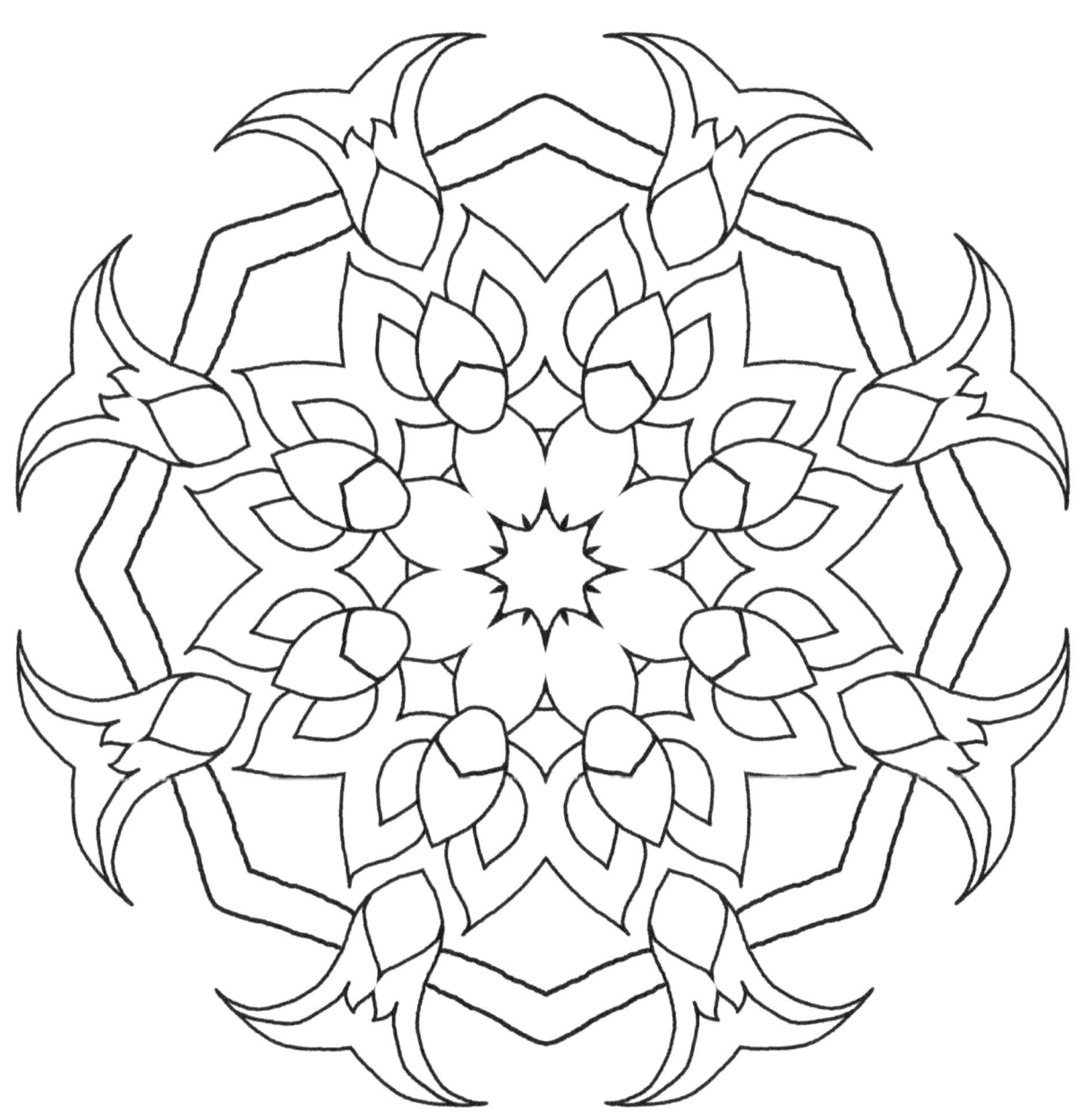

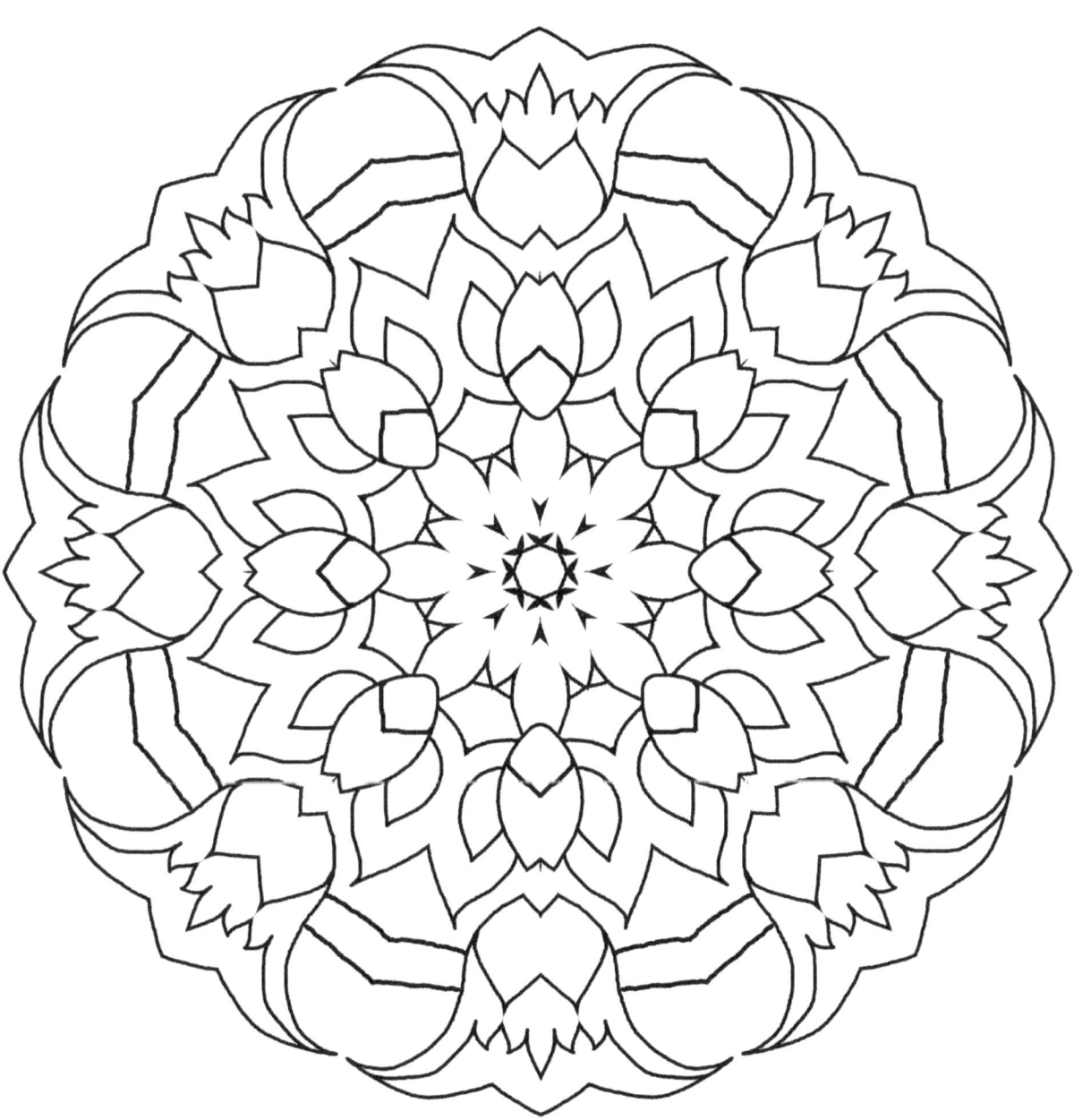

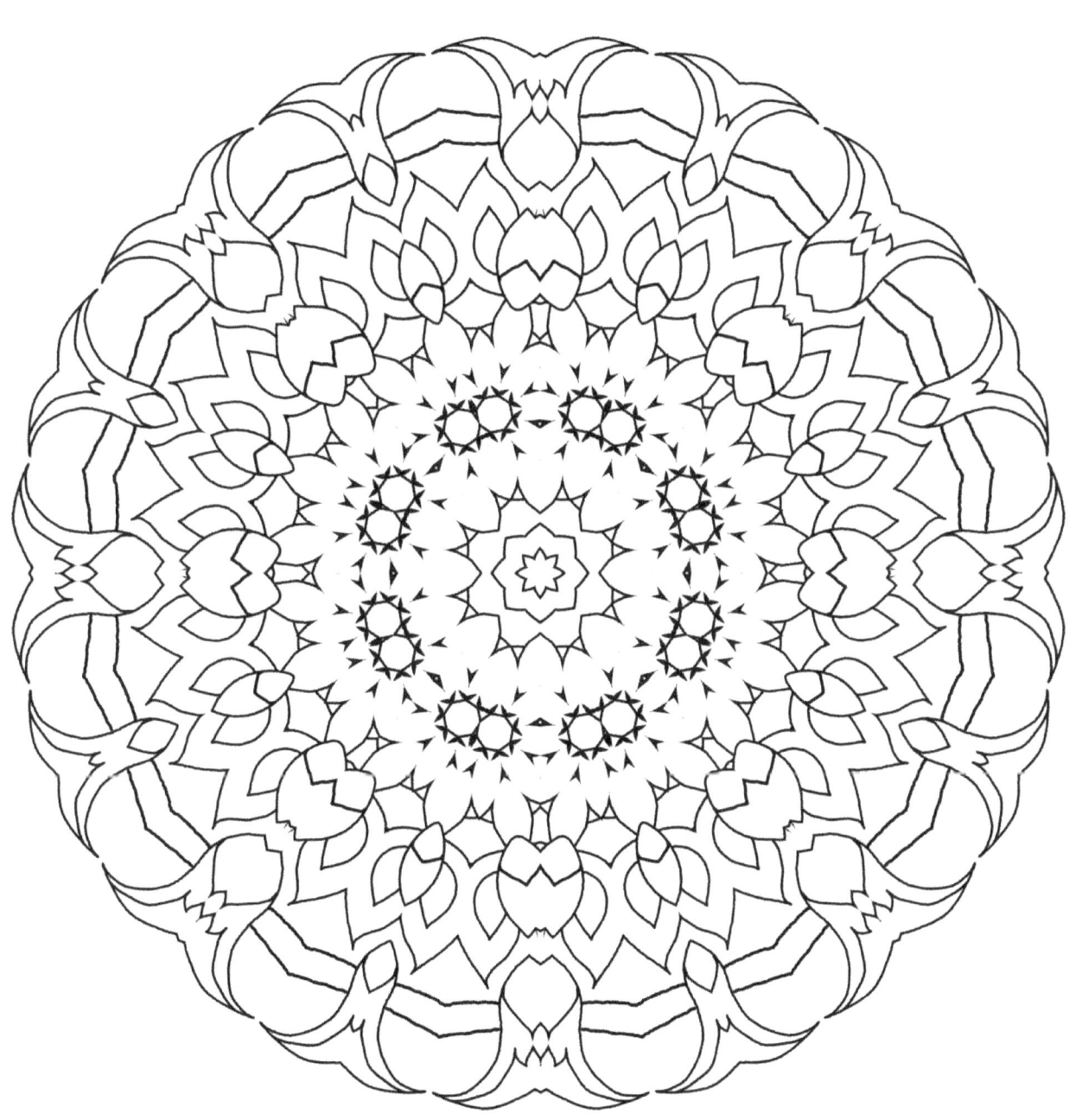

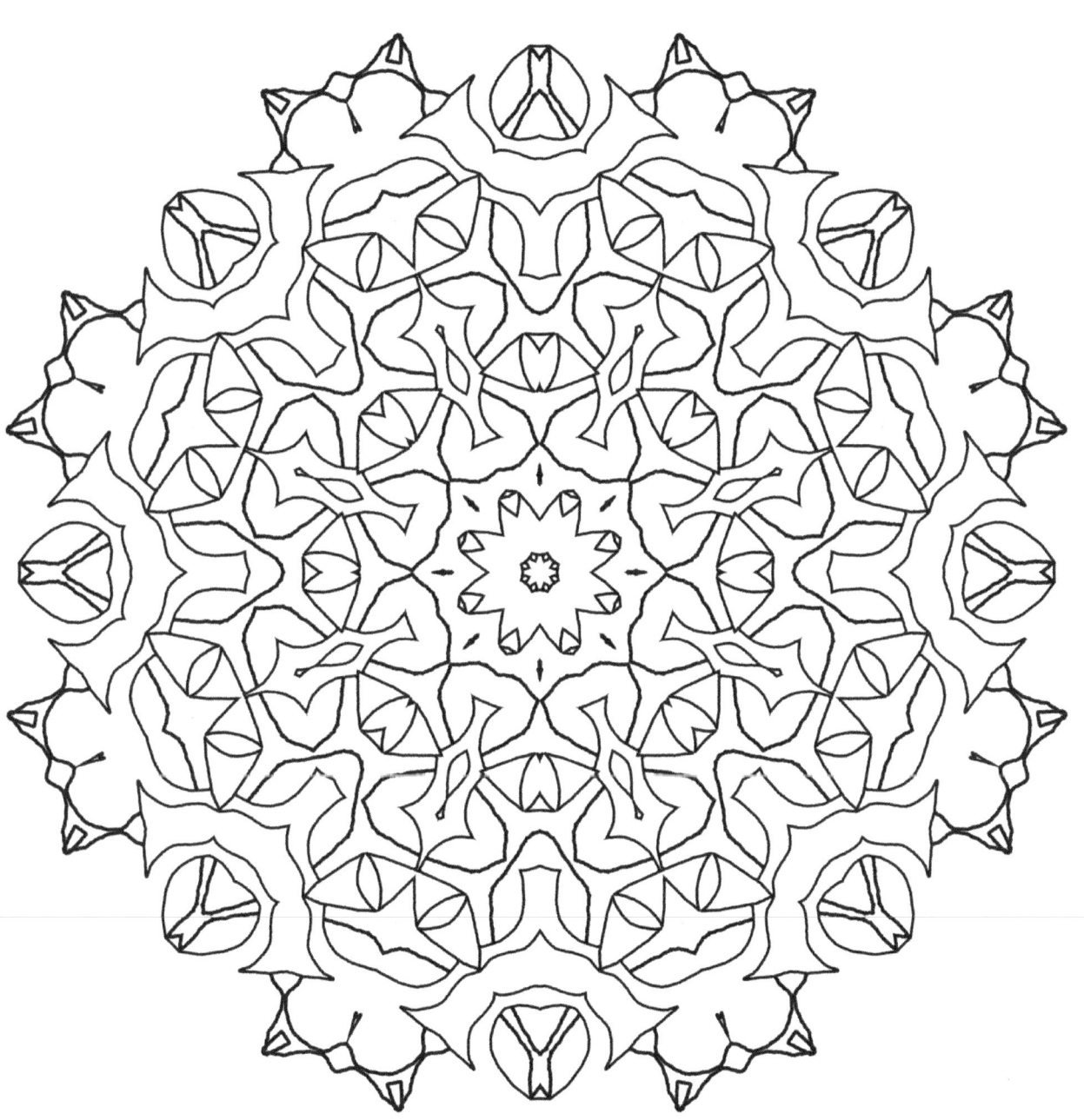

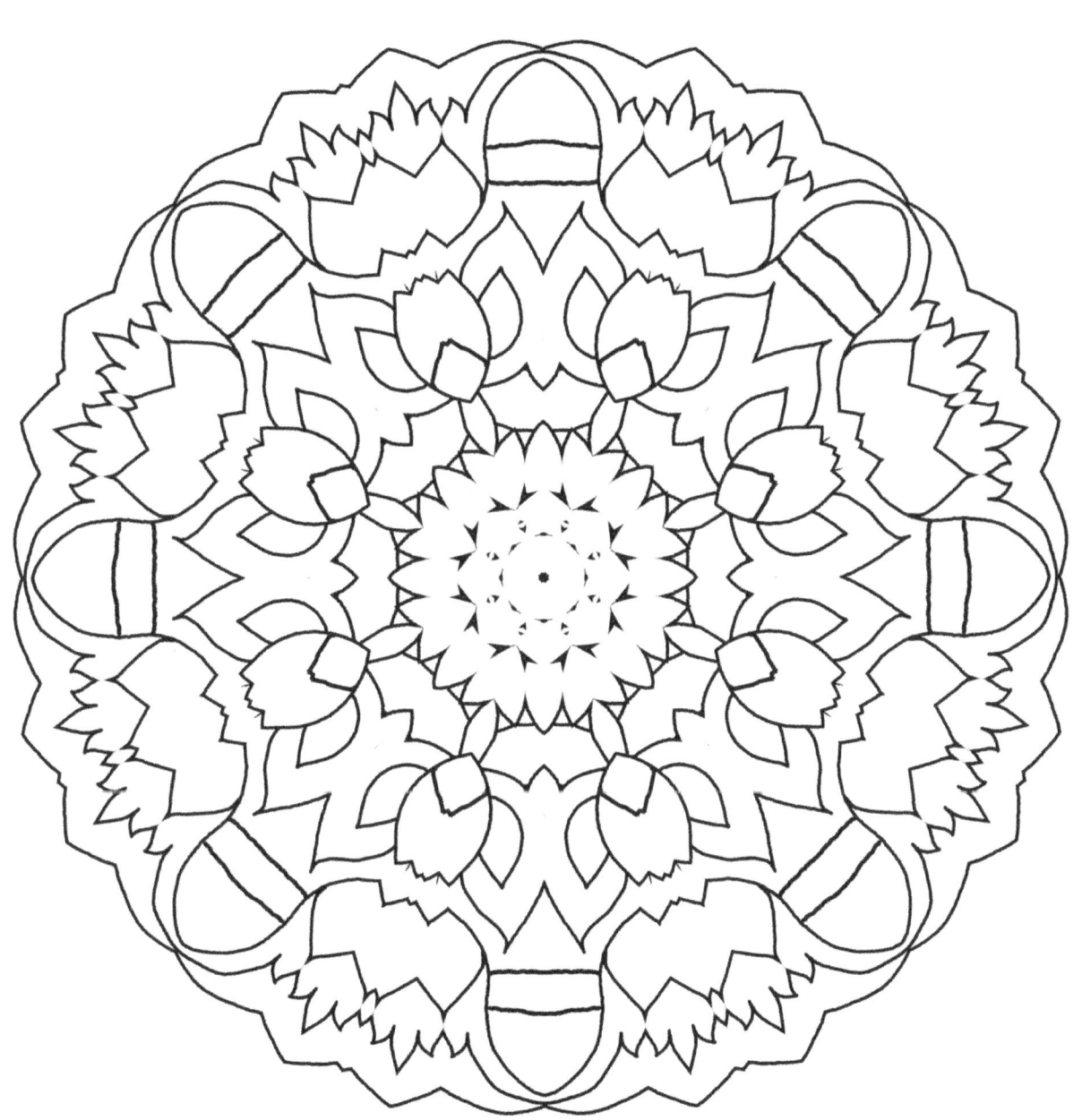

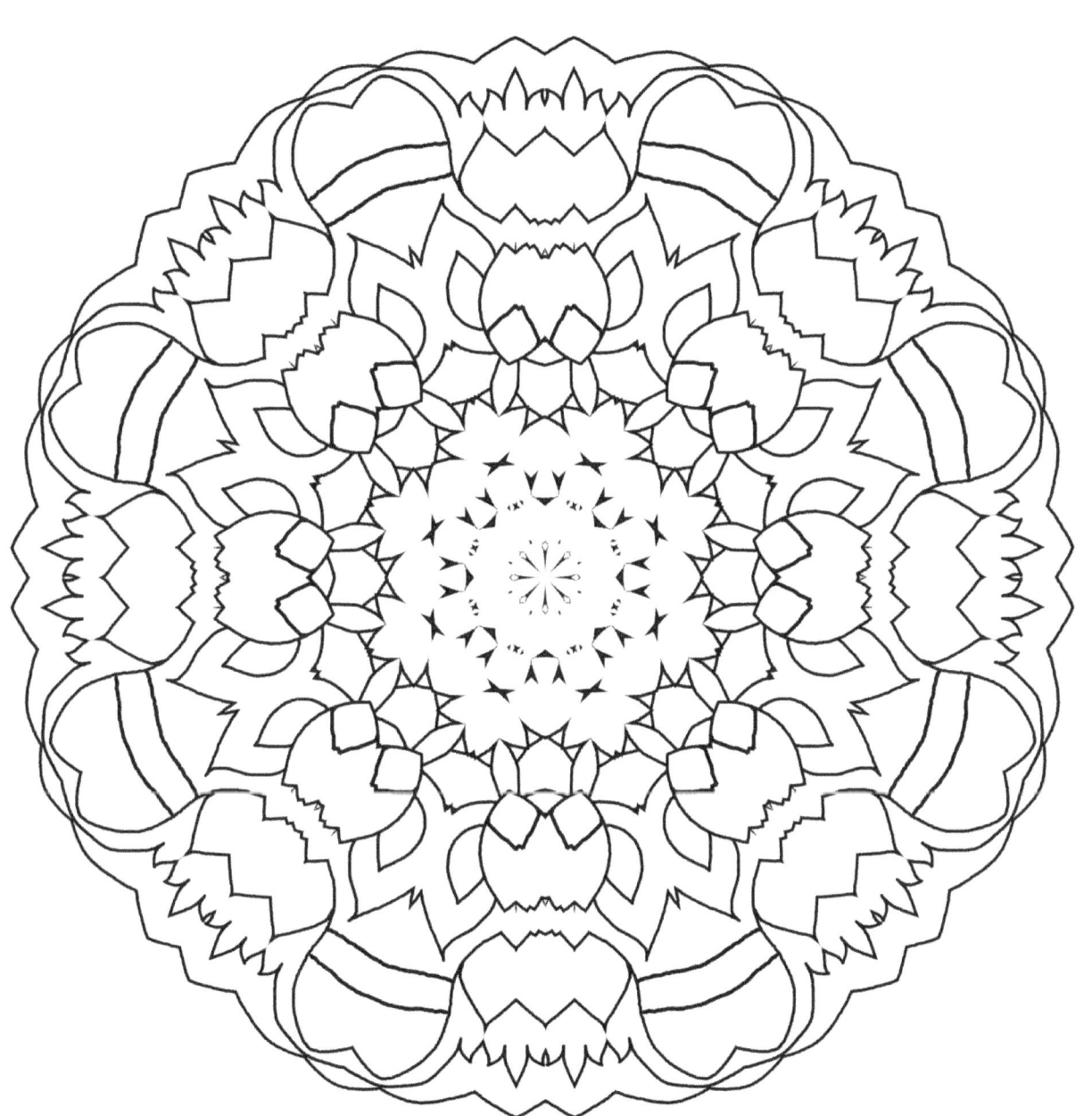

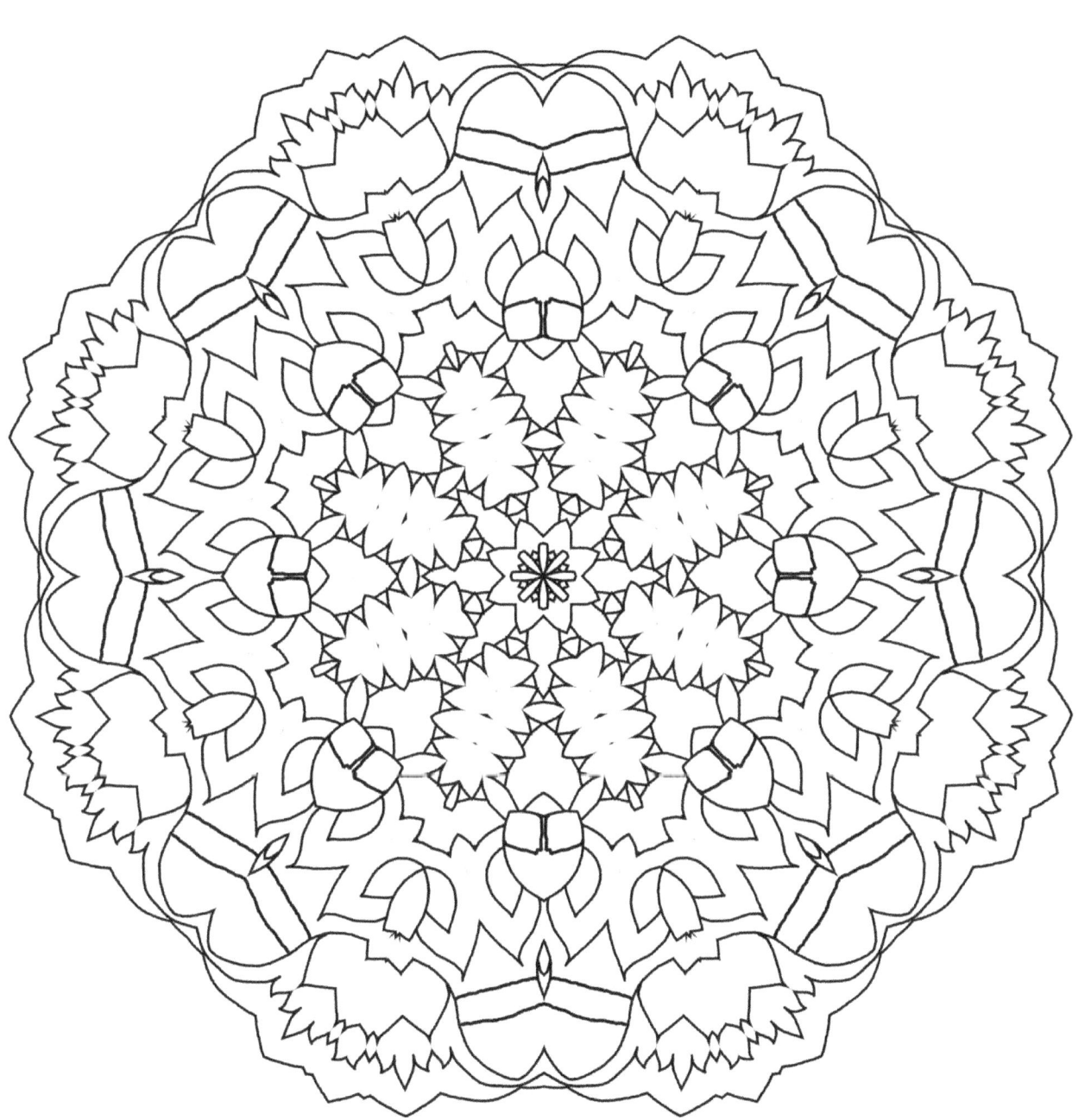

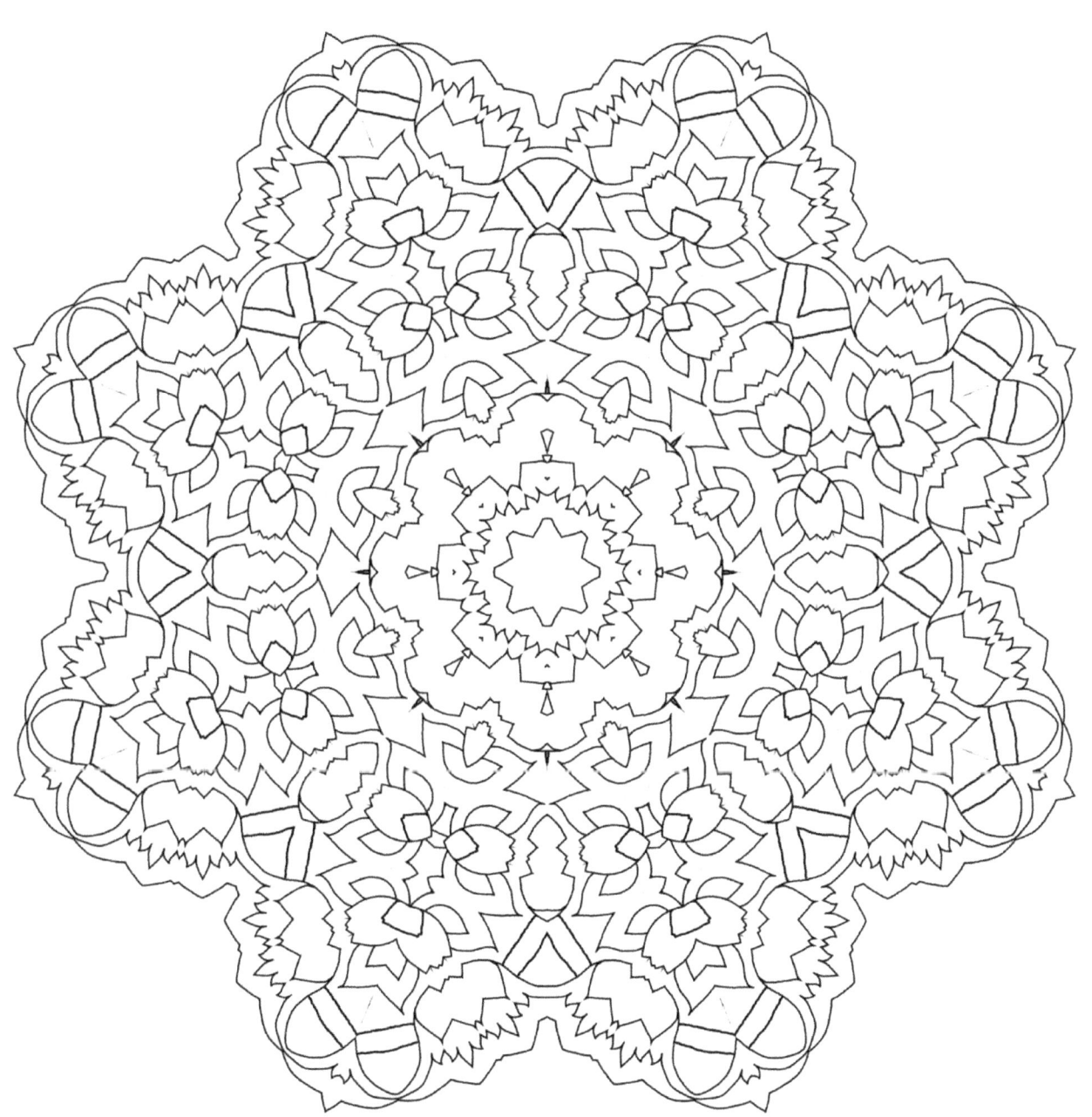

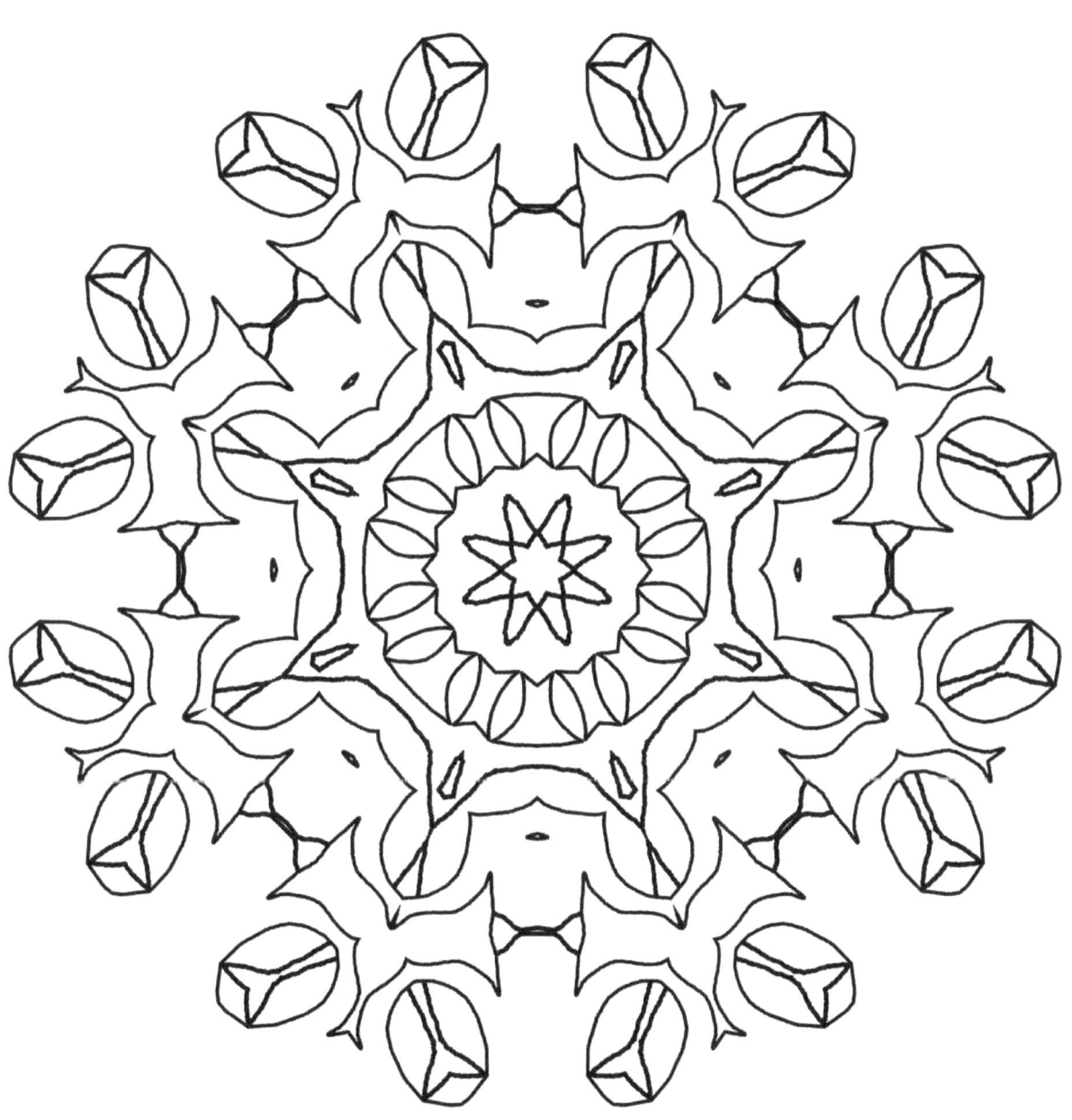

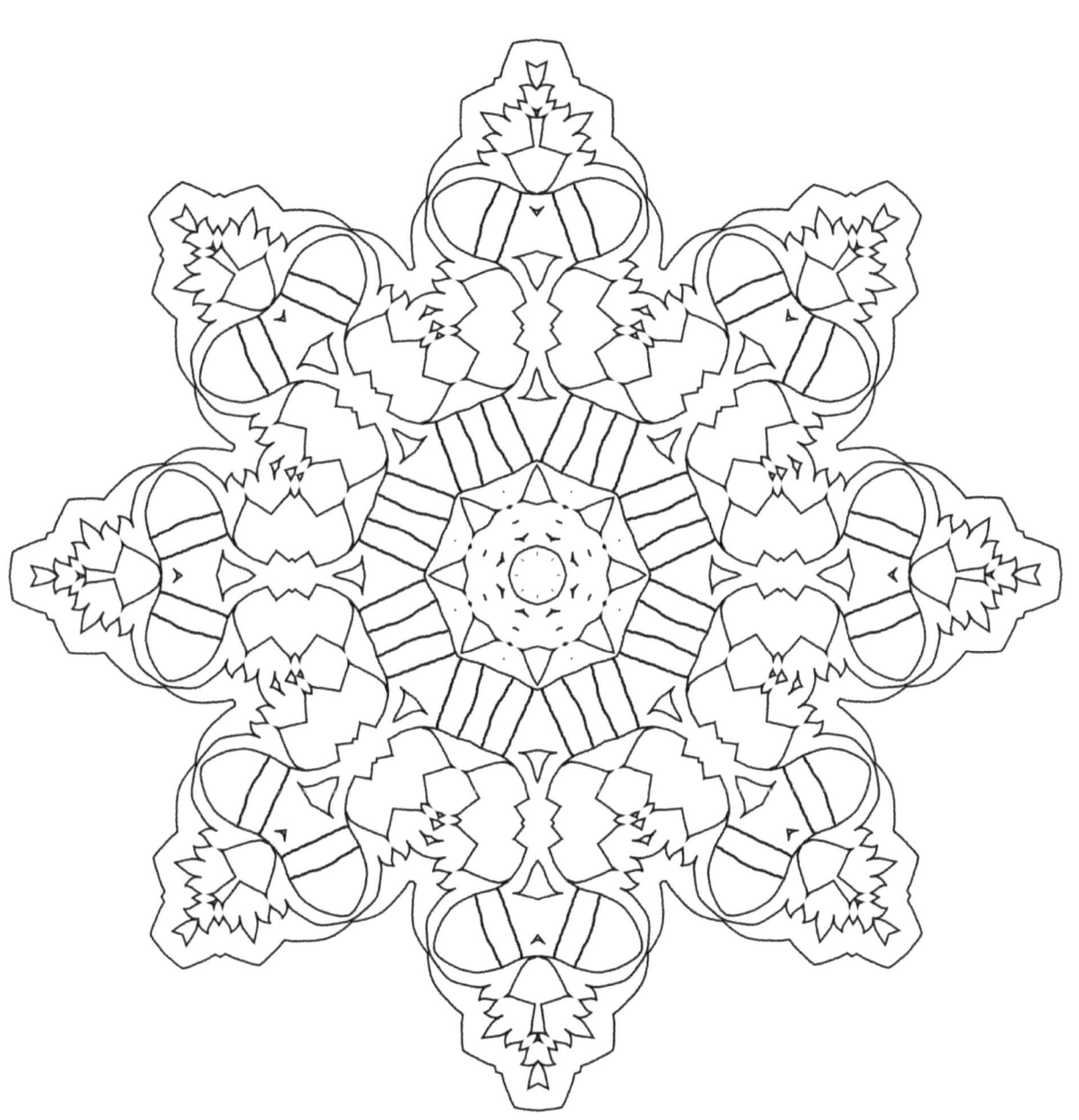

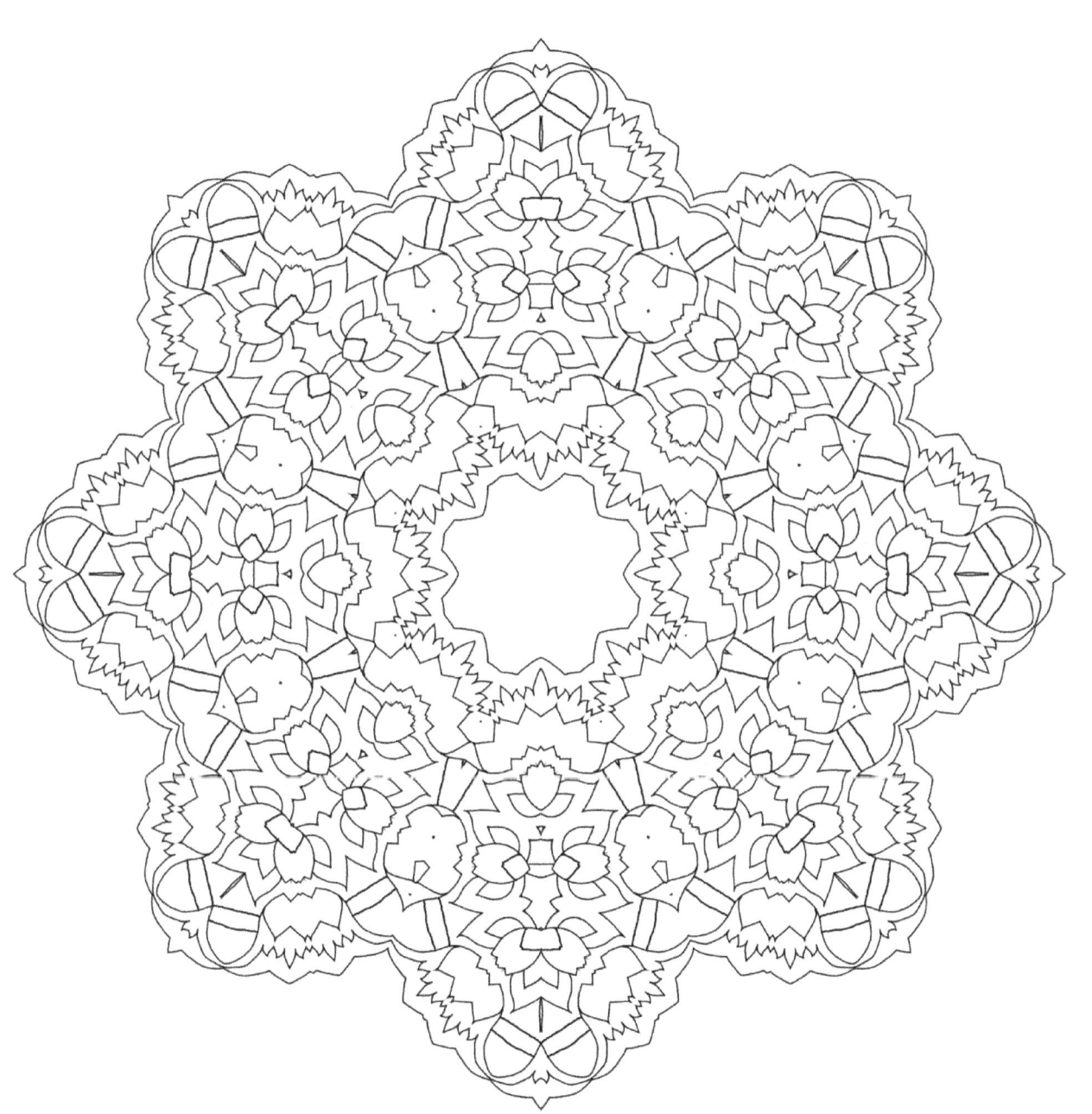

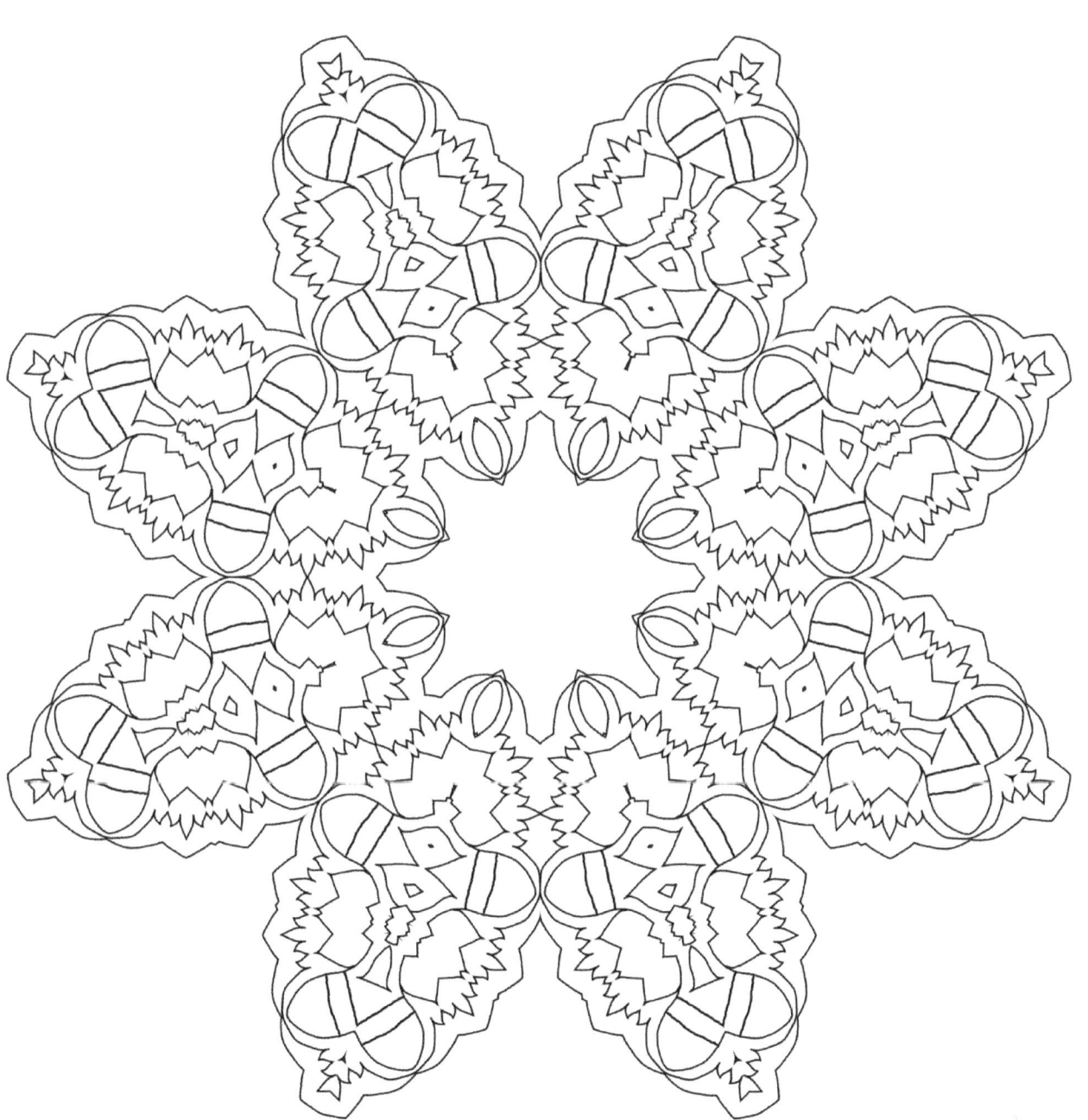

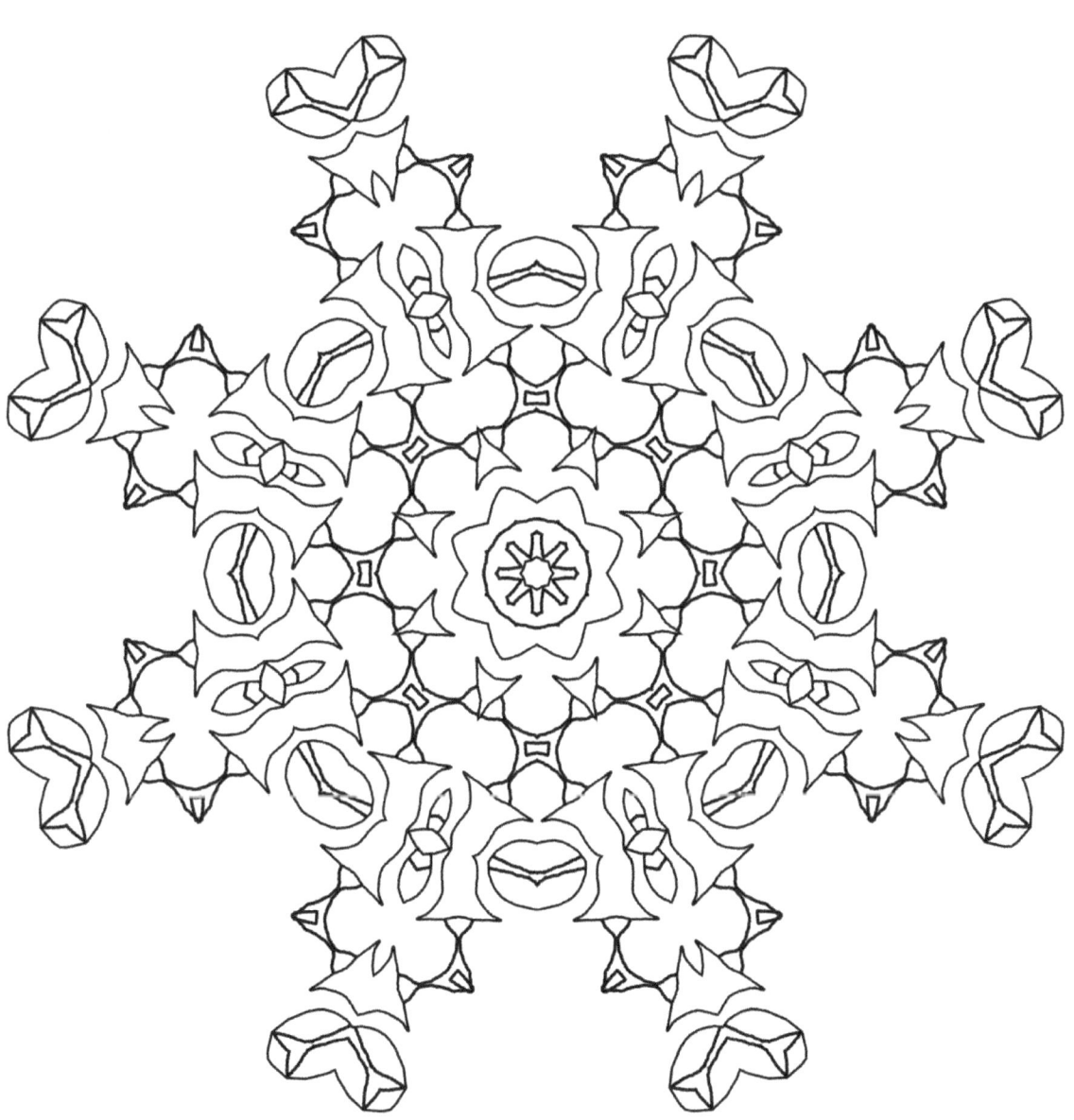

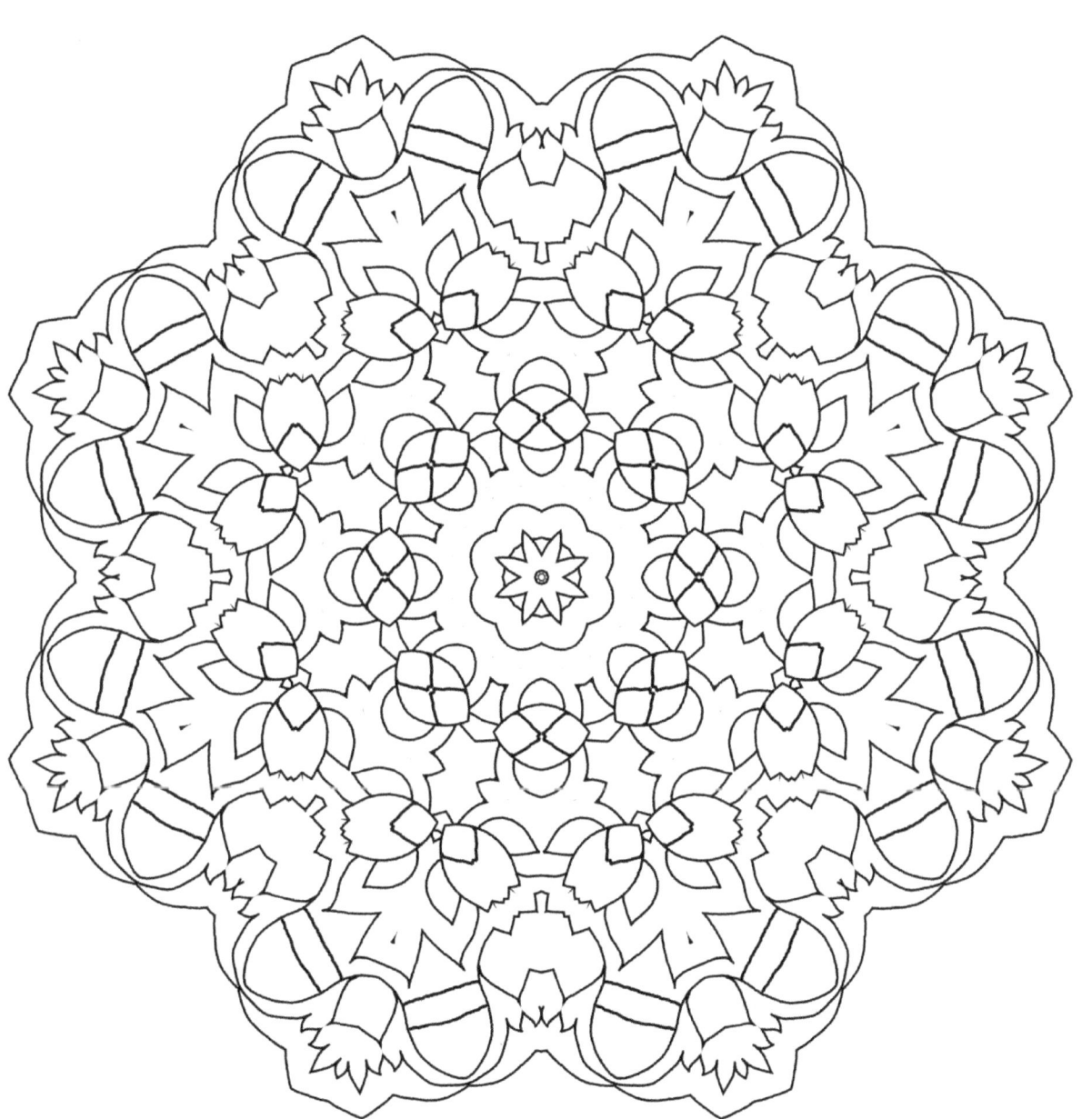

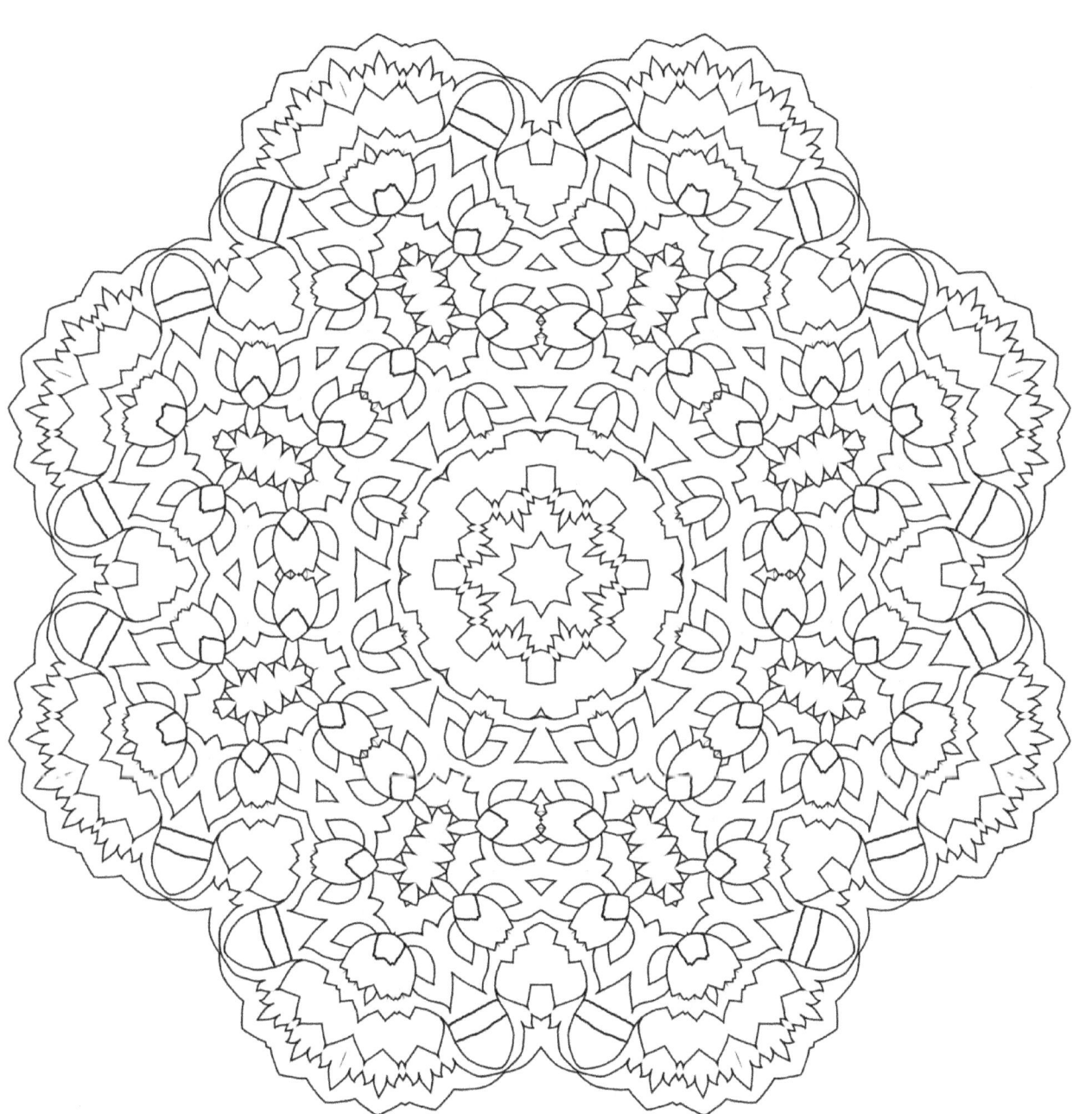

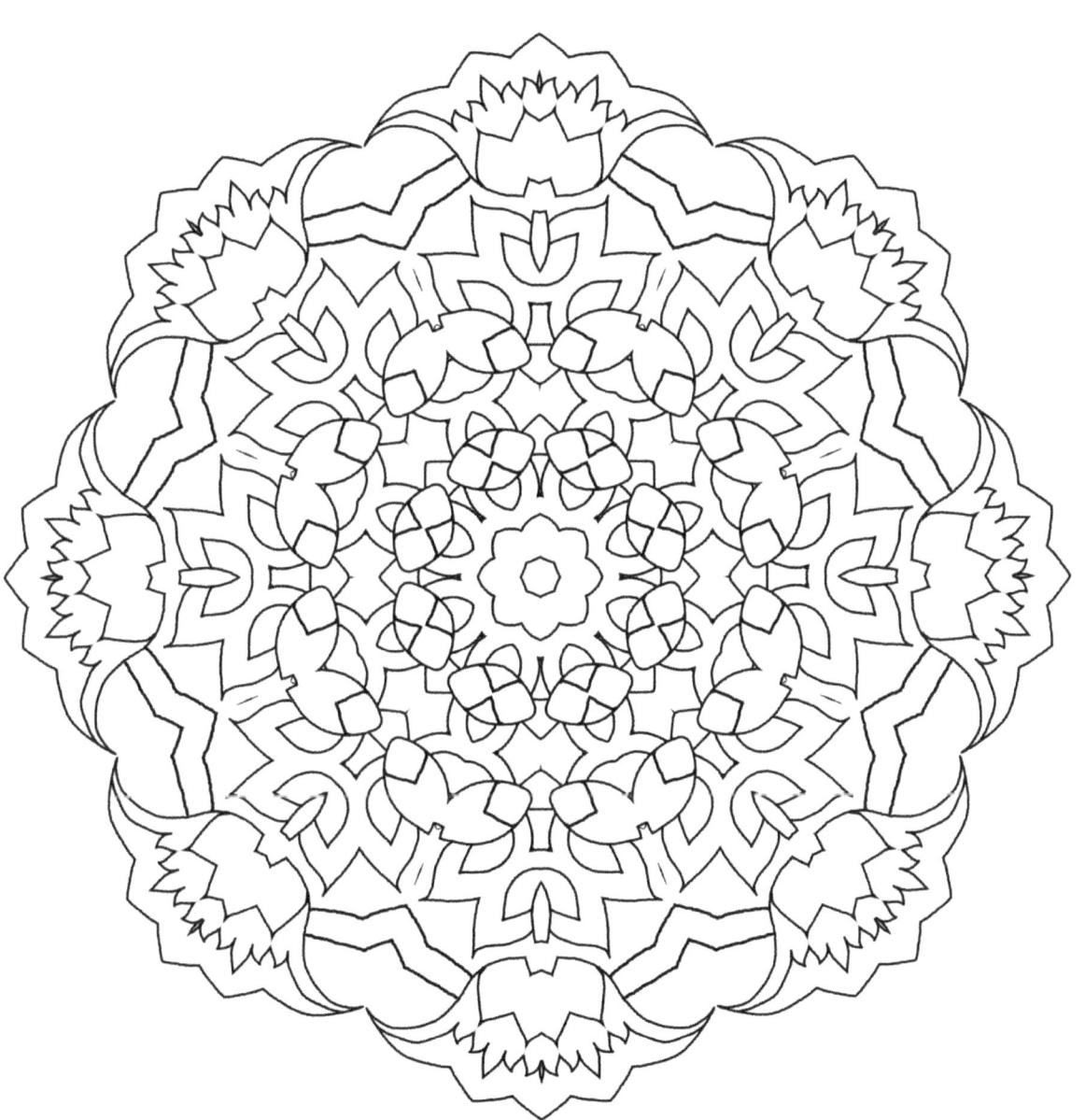

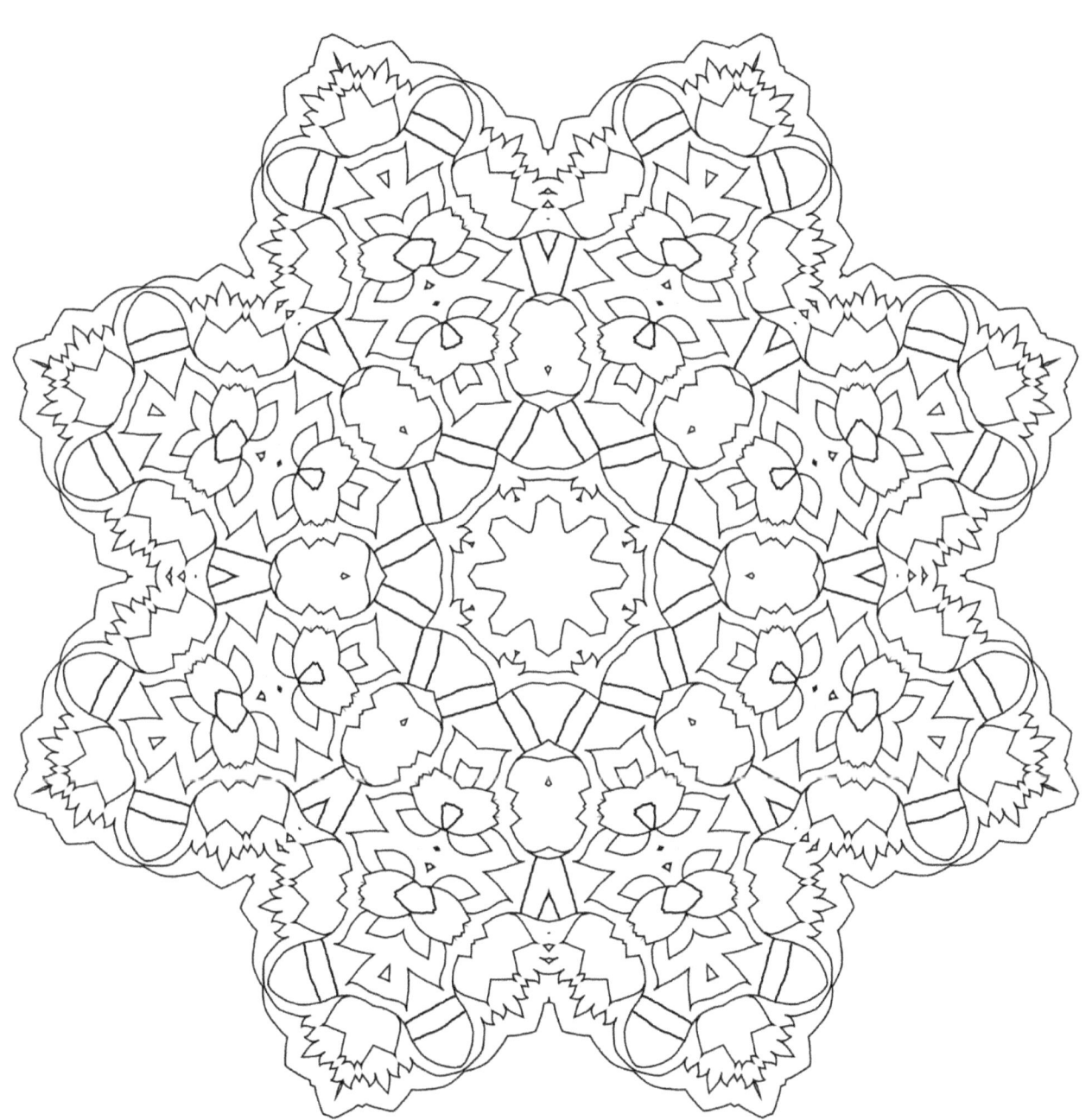

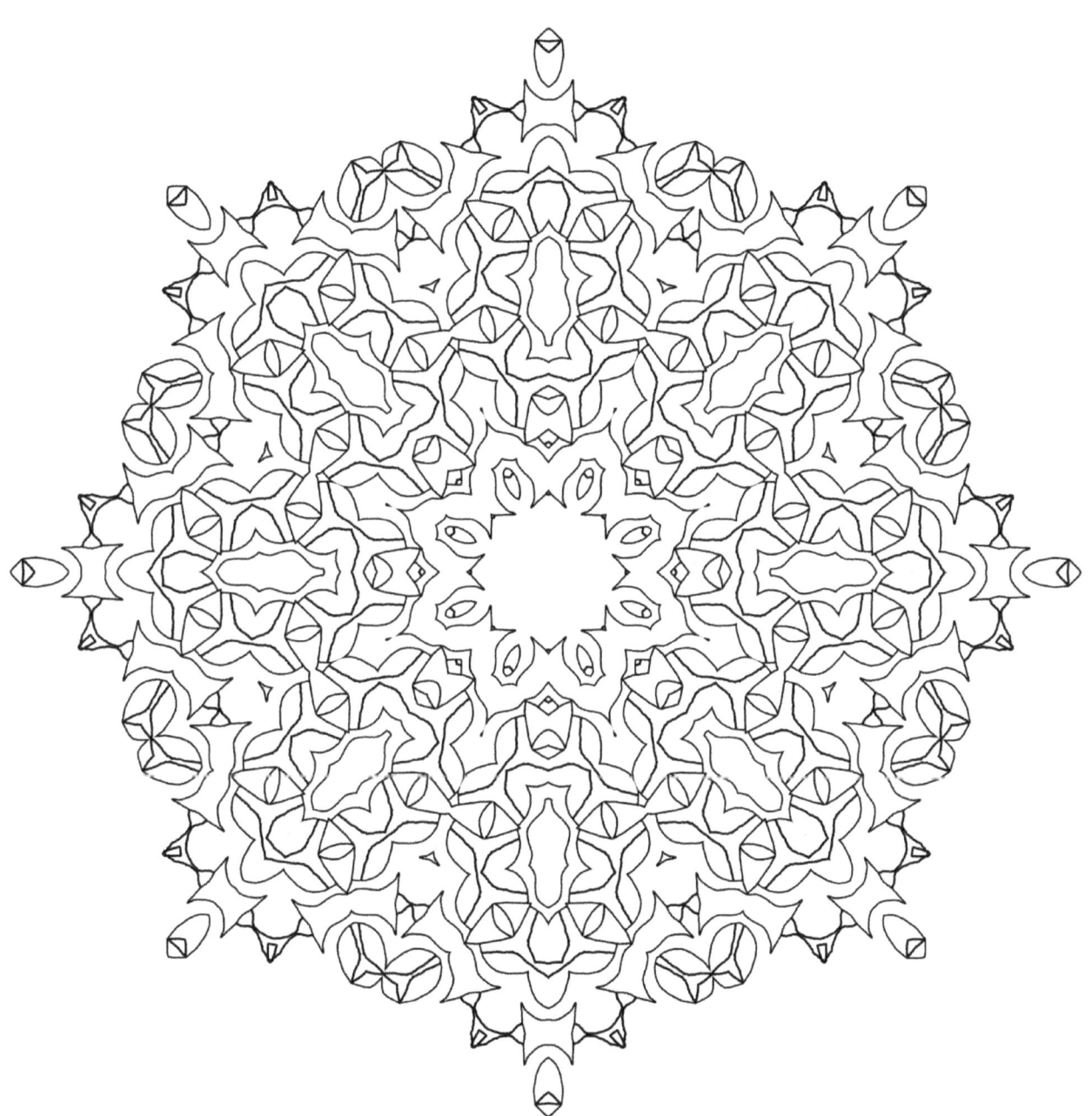

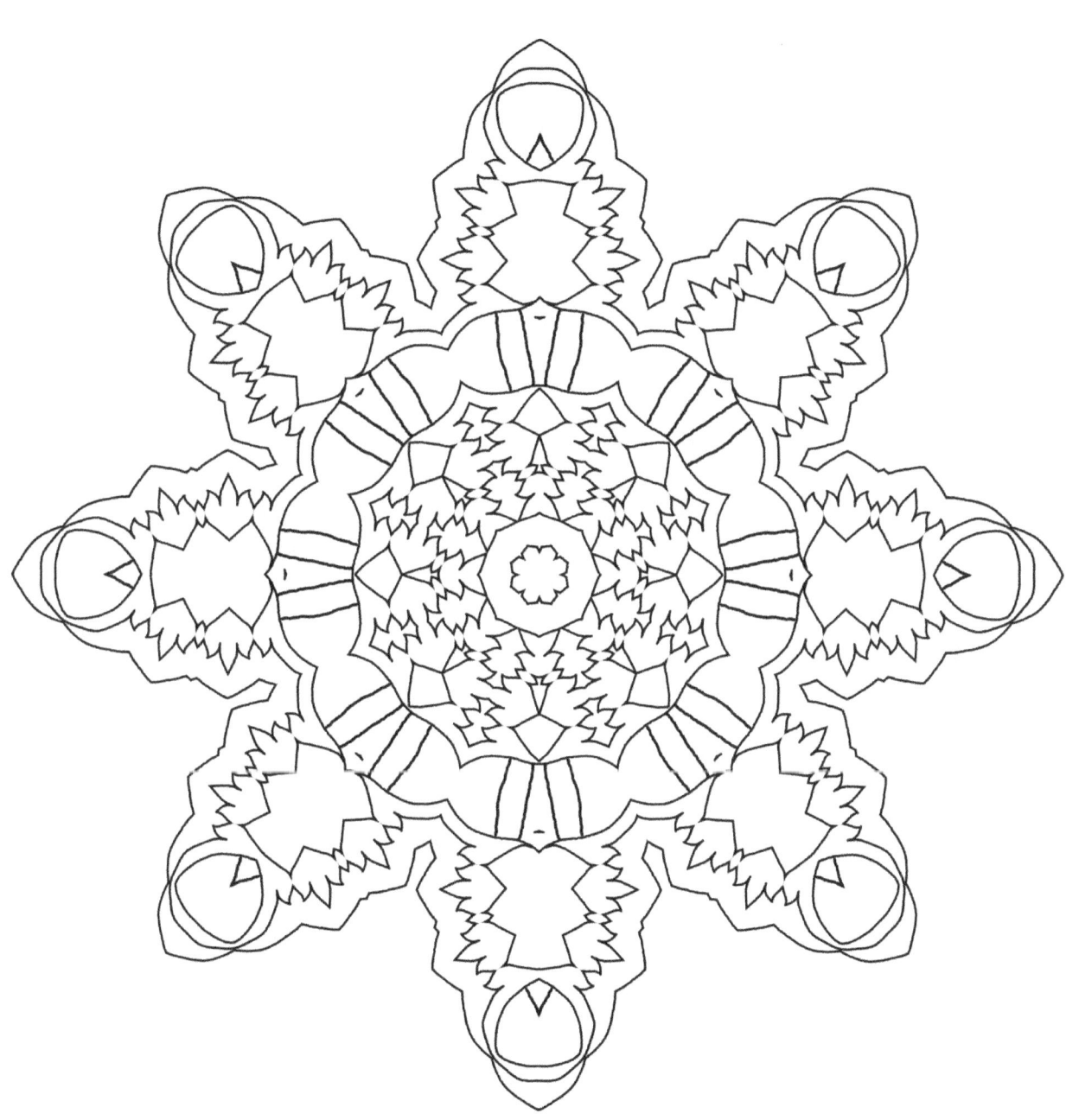

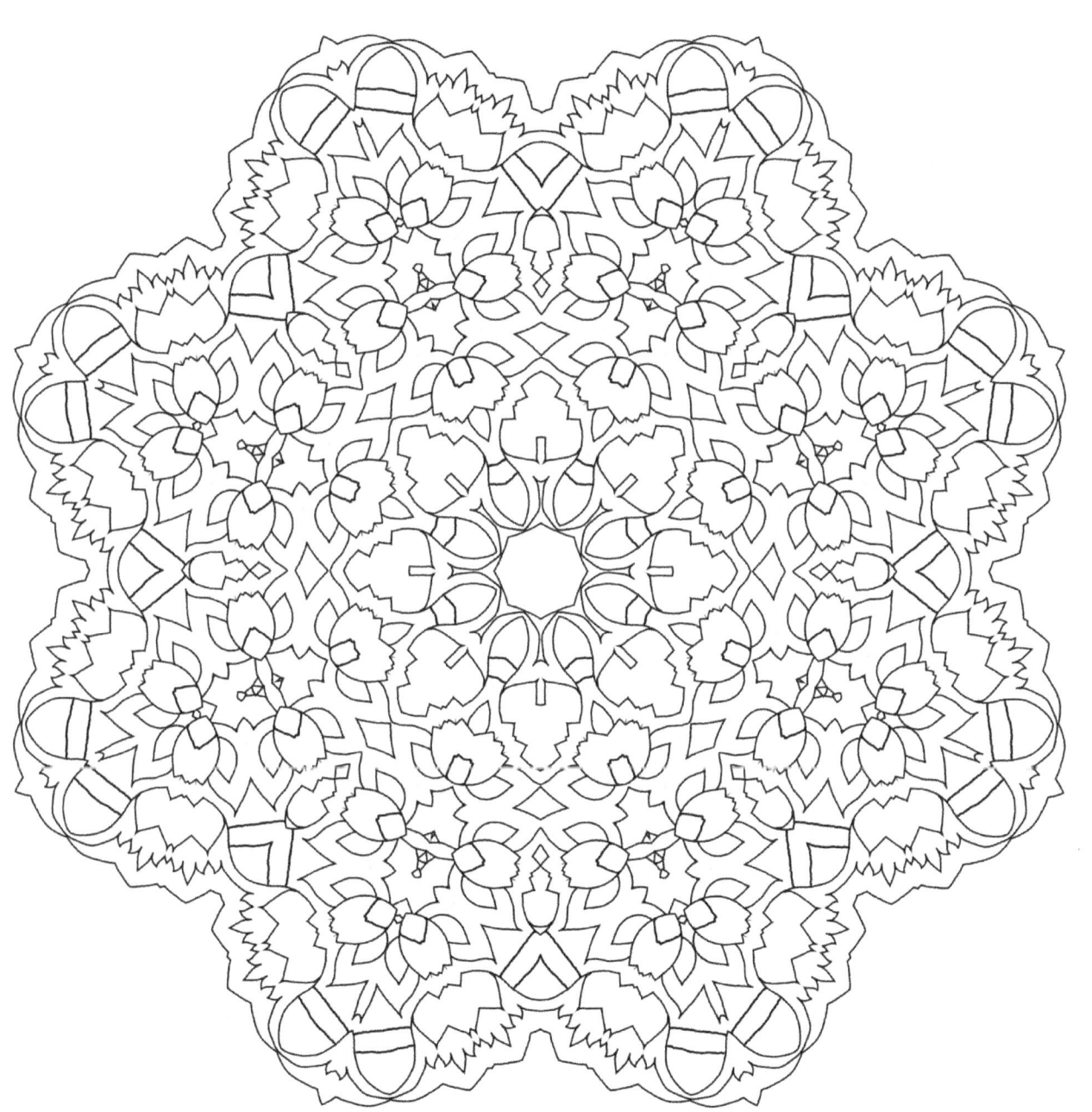

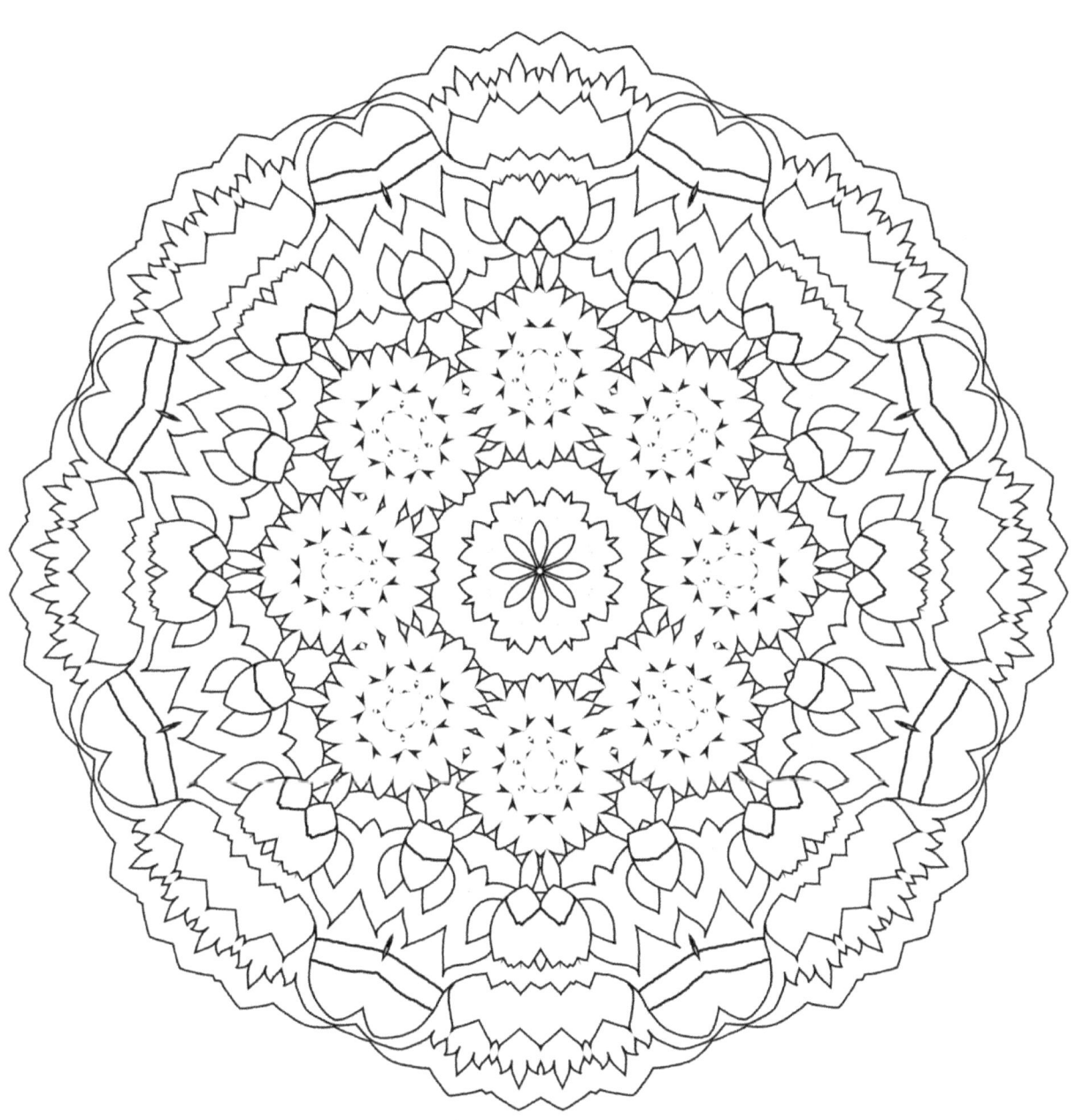

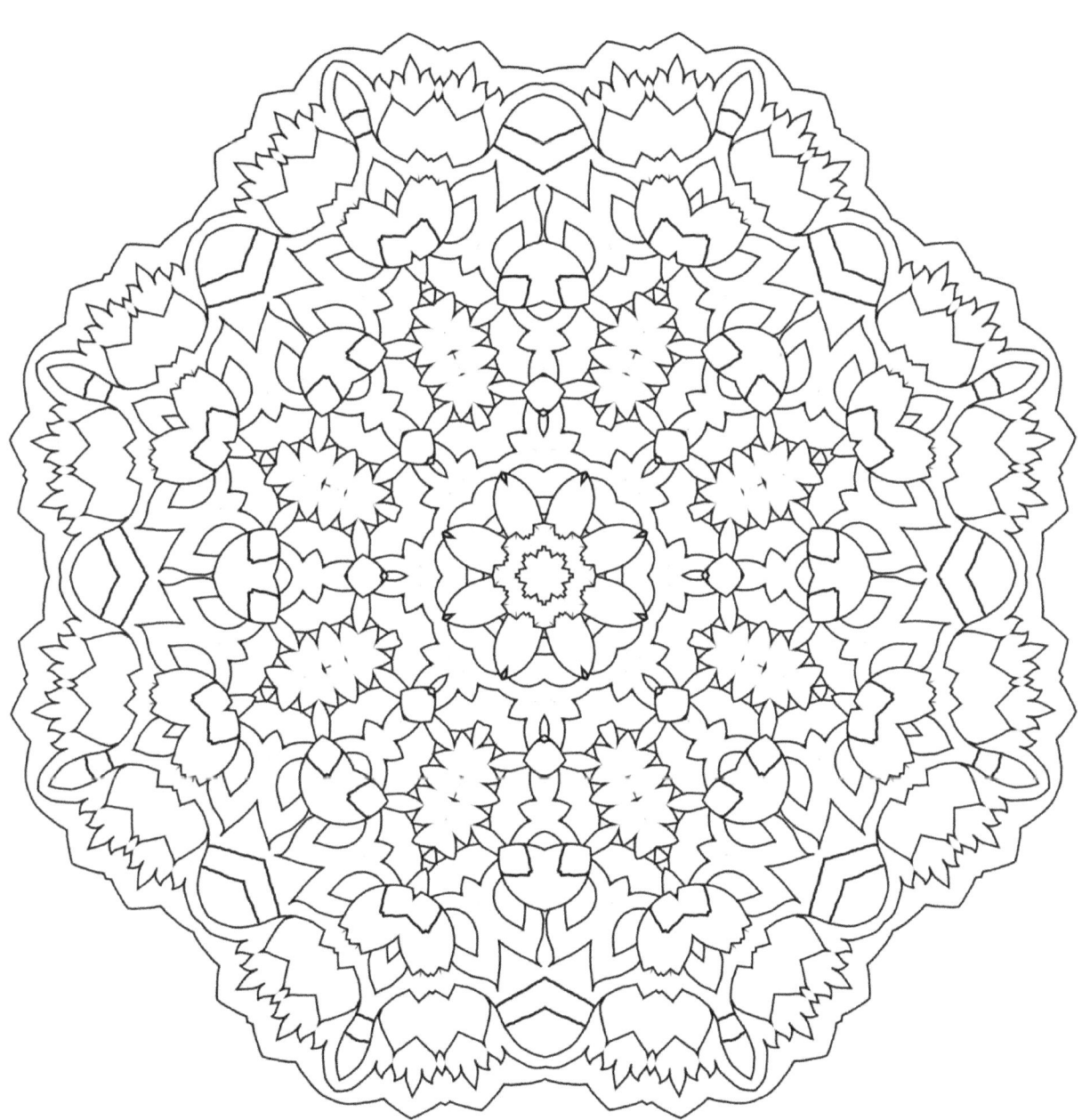

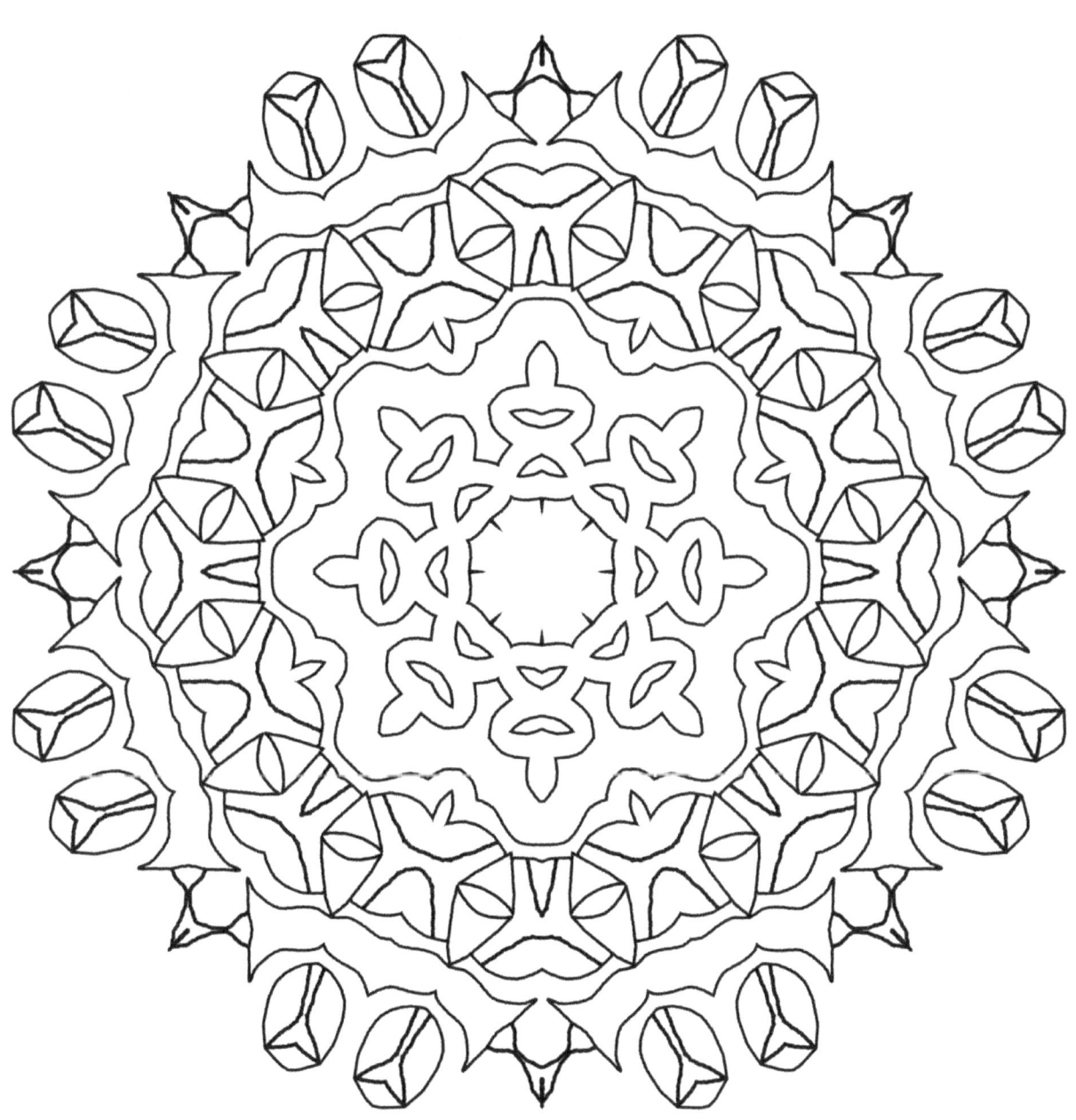

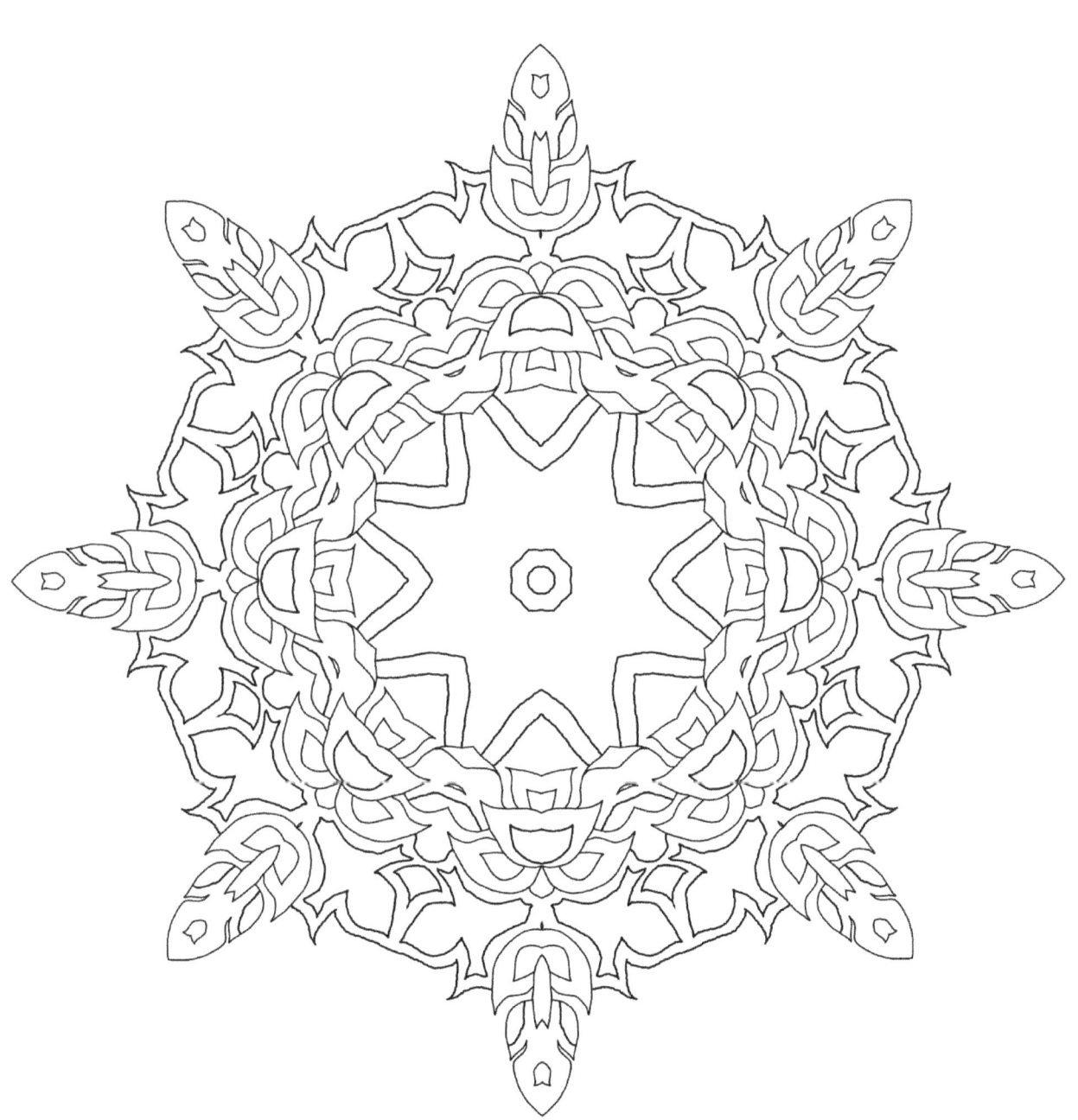

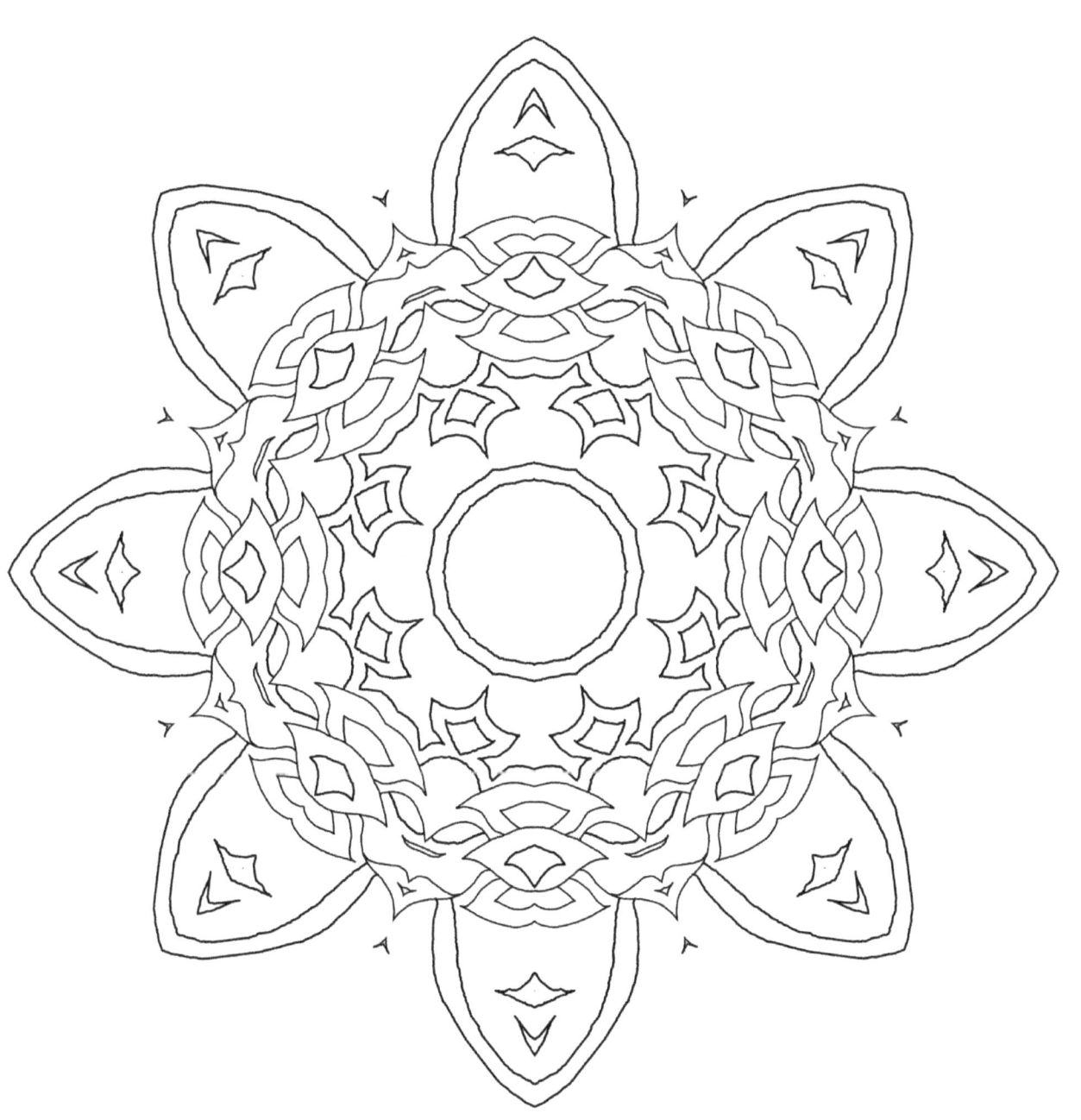

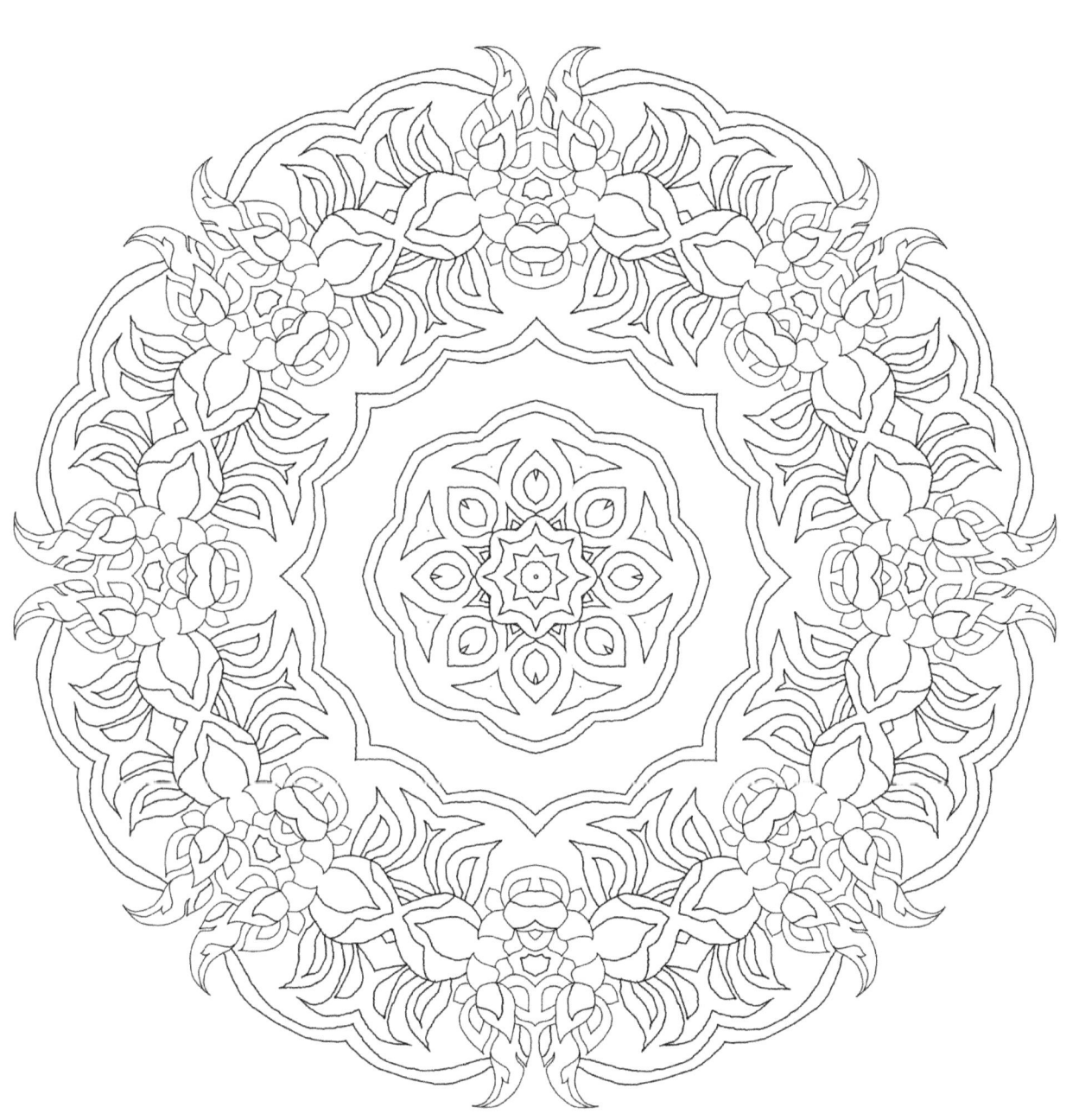

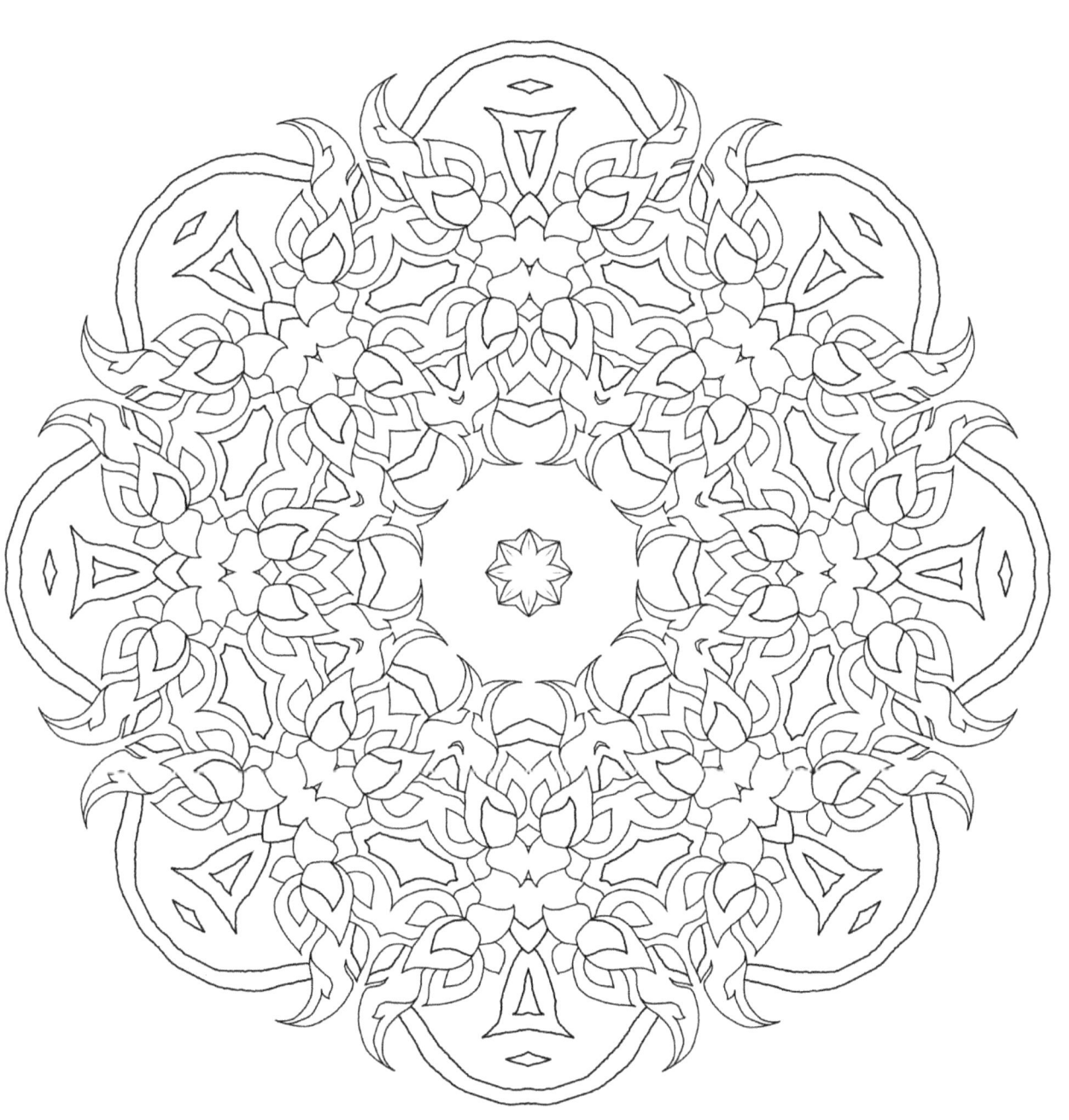

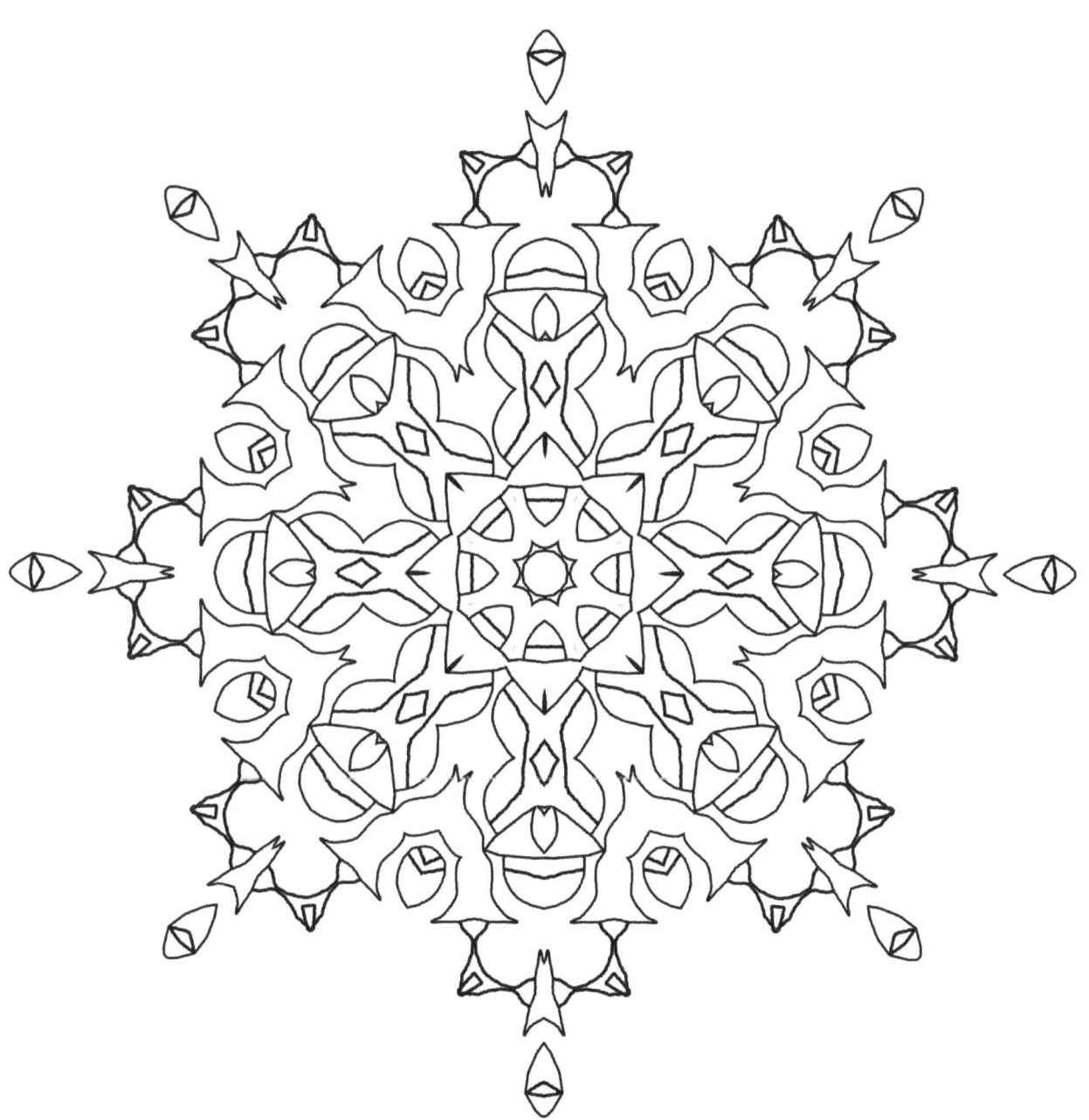

Thank you

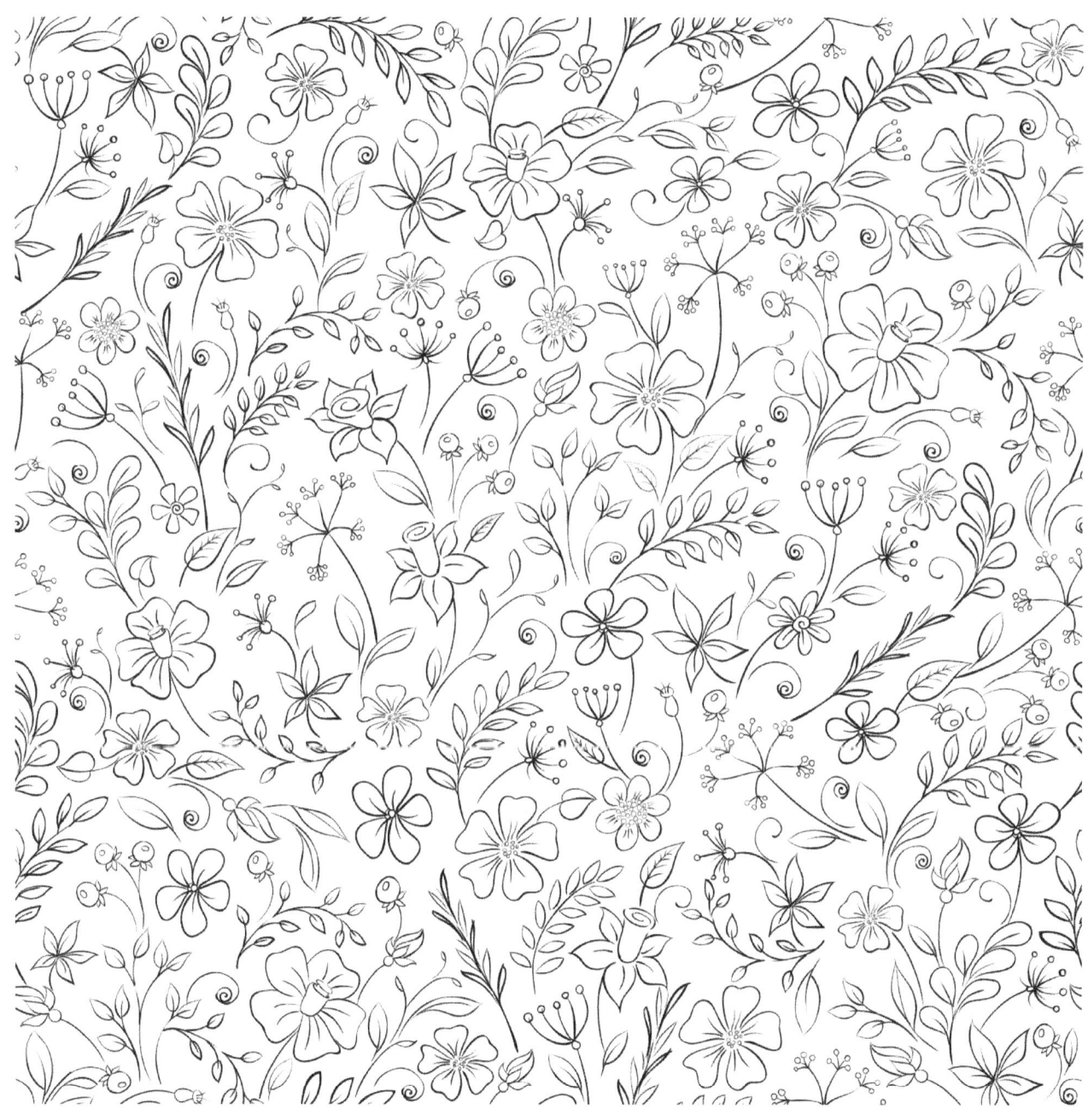

www.ingramcontent.com/pod-product-compliance
Lightning Source LLC
Chambersburg PA
CBHW081115180526

45170CB00008B/2861